THE STRANGEST HUMAN SEX CEREMONIES AND CUSTOMS

J. Talalaj & S. Talalaj

Hill of Content
Melbourne

First published in Australia 1994
by Hill of Content Publishing Co Pty Ltd
86 Bourke Street Melbourne 3000 Australia

© J. Talalaj 1994
Cover Photograph taken by Emil Schulthess from his book 'Africa'
(Maness Verlag, Conzett & Huber, Zurich 1958).
Typeset by Midland Typesetters, Maryborough Victoria
Printed by SNP Offset (M) Sdn. Bhd.
National Library of Australia
Cataloguing-in-Publication data

Talalaj, Janusz Joseph.
  The strangest human sex ceremonies and customs.

  Bibliography.
  Includes index.
  ISBN 0 85572 247 9.

  1. Rites and ceremonies. 2. Manners and customs. I. Title

390

The publisher and author would like to thank the following for
permission to use the specified photographs.
Phallic procession in Japan, Ian L. McQueen
Aboriginal witch doctor, Australian Collectors Choice
                        Murray Views,
                        Gympie, Queensland
The Living Goddess reproduced by kind permission
of Berlitz Publishing Co. Ltd. London

Contents

Preface

This book offers a unique survey of the most bizarre and fascinating aspects of human behaviour. We believe that in this book, so full of adventure and suspense, the reader will find many descriptions almost impossible to grasp as true.

The reader will find, for instance, how in some cultures, for the pleasure of women, men mutilated their penises and inserted a wide range of devices into the glans. Equally startling were the requirements for being 'beautiful' and sexually attractive among women. Truk Islanders had the custom of extending a girl's vulva and to demonstrate her sexuality, a Truk girl inserted tinkling objects into the pierced labia minor. The objects rang when the girl walked and demonstrated her sexuality. Descriptions of the most amazing marriages are also to be found and the reasoning behind these customs, such as marriage to a fruit or a ghost, is explained.

Many of the customs and celebrations described in the book still tend to be closely guarded secrets by the people who practise or used to practise them. Now, in the late twentieth century, every nation or tribe would like others to know that they always had only compassionate and 'wise' customs. In order to avoid 'offending' them, most books about various countries (particularly travel books) tend to omit these customs. We disagree with this approach. In our view we should not hide from the real history of humanity and should not reshape history simply to feel good.

However, one should not argue that there were people who had better or worse customs. Cruel and indecent customs were practised with the same zeal in Europe as in other parts of the world. Human sacrifice was practised in Europe, phallic worship was a part of European culture and phallic trophy was not something confined to a region in Africa but also cherished in parts of Europe. That similar customs can be observed in various parts of the world, among peoples who had no contact with each other, shows that in reality we are *one* people and that these are *our* customs.

This book is about our present and past and it is dedicated to everyone who wants to fully understand mankind without any bias.

In closing we would like to thank the countless people who entertained us worldwide and helped us understand better their unique culture. We would also like to thank Mrs Daniela Talalaj for her help in researching the book. We would also like to thank our publisher Michelle Anderson for her efforts in making this book more attractive.

J & S Talalaj

1.

Incredible Sexual Stimulation

The Best Lover

In some cultures men mutilated their penises for the pleasure of women. This custom was particularly common among the Dayaks of Borneo, despite the fact that it involved a painful operation with a silver needle. The needle was inserted into the glans of the penis and left until the resulting opening had properly healed, forming a channel through the glans.

A man who possessed such a channel could then insert various objects into the glans. They would become instruments of pleasure for his sexual partner. These 'decorations' varied from ivory or metal rods to ingenious contrivances ending in brushes or tiny bristles. The devices were said to greatly stimulate a woman during intercourse.

The Dayaks were proud of their penis decorations, saying that they gave their women great pleasure. Although it was the man who decorated his penis, women were said to be the inventors of the most sophisticated devices for their own sexual pleasure.

Some men had more than one channel in their penises, enabling them to attach several embellishments at the same time. With such a multitude of penis devices a man was said to be the best lover. Such men were especially admired and women made great efforts to have them as a lover or husband.

Women often indicated to their lovers the kind of objects and the sizes they desired for love-making. It was customary among Dayak women to roll a cigarette of tobacco leaf of a particular shape and size to indicate her preference; the message was readily understood by a potential lover.

Similar customs prevailed in North Celebes in Indonesia. Local men used to decorate their sexual organs with the eyelids of a goat. The eyelids, including the extensive eyelashes, were tied around the glans for women's pleasure.

In Sumatra, Batta tribe members had a different custom. They inserted minute pieces of metal or stones under the foreskin of the penis to increase the friction power of the erect penis. They believed this greatly enhanced women's pleasure during intercourse. The Araucarian Indians of Argentina used to attach minute brushes made of horse hair to their glans for the same purpose.

Women in Bali did not favour mechanical devices on their lovers; instead they inserted various small objects into their vagina to enhance their pleasure during love-making. The most commonly used were the leaves of the mugwort (*Artemisia vulgaris*).

The Indian sex manual, the famous Kama Sutra also recommended certain devices called 'apadravyas' as an addition to the male member for the purpose of enhancing excitement during coitus. These embellishments of the penis were made of gold, iron or silver. Wood or buffalo horn or even ivory could also be used.

The devices were supposed to take the form of bracelets to fit both the penis and the vulva of the intending lovers. The most common device was called jalaka. It was a 'tube open at both ends, with a hole through it, outwardly rough and studded with soft globules, and made to fit the size of the yoni [vagina] and tied to the waist . . .'

The Kama Sutra says that such devices 'can be used in connection with the penis or in place of it'. In addition to devices which can be easily attached to the penis, Kama Sutra also advises men to make perforations through the glans in a way similar to the Dayaks. It recommends the following technique: 'In the hole made in the lingam [phallus] a man may put apadravyas of various forms such as the "round", the wooden mortar, the flower, the lock of hair, the bone of the heron, and other things named according to their forms and means of using them'.

Correcting Nature

From time to time people all over the world have invented various ways to sexually arouse their partners. The most creative in this respect seem to be the people of the Micronesian island of Ponape. As late as the mid 1970s it was reported that the job of sexual stimulation was performed by a tiny sex worker, namely a local variety of a stinging ant native to the island. The male lover placed the ant on the clitoris of his partner and the sting of the ant was said to produce a short but acute tinglingly erotic sensation.

This, however is not the end of Ponape inventions. In another procedure the male partner is said to place a small fish into his partner's vagina, which he then gradually licks out before commencing intercourse. It has not been confirmed, however, whether this latter report is the description of a practice or a piece of folklore.

Long ago some Korean women used an ingenious but cruel way to sexually stimulate a tired husband. They jabbed his testicles with a pin.

Years ago men realised that women would be greatly sexually aroused by a man with a large penis. However, significantly enlarging the penis appears to be an impossible task. Not so for the Topinamba of Brazil in the sixteenth century. They accomplished it by encouraging poisonous snakes to bite the penis. As a result the men were in pain for about half a year, but their penises became monstrously big and they were convinced that the suffering was worth while since the women were so delighted.

'Burning' Love

The inhabitants of Truk Island (Micronesia) had truly revolting sexual customs. Local women deliberately caused painful burns to their lovers during sexual intercourse in order to have more pleasure.

A woman placed a small portion of powdered breadfruit stump on the skin of her sexual partner and then ignited the powder. This not only caused an acute burn pain but also left an ugly scar on the lover's body. Under the influence of western civilisation the procedure was later 'improved' by employing cigarettes. The loving woman used to light the cigarette to burn the skin of a man. During just one bout a woman could produce several 'hot spots' on the arms of her lover, but the usual number of burns was about six.

In return, the men used to perform a rather gentle mutilation of their partner's body during intercourse. They scratched the woman's cheek with their long thumbnails which were deliberately grown long for this purpose. But compared with the scratches inflicted by males, the technique employed by women was far more advanced in its cruelty. Strangely, both partners were happy with this unusual sexual stimulation. It is exceptional, since in no other society has there been the custom of deliberately inflicting burns during copulation.

Inflicting pain during sexual intercourse was not confined to Truks. Trobriands used to scratch each other while making love. Trobriands and inhabitants of the island of Ponape (Micronesia) had another curious custom; biting the eyebrows during love-making. An even stranger custom was practised by Choroti, a tribe in Central South America who used to spit on each other's face while engaging in sexual intercourse.

Cruel Courtship

Courtship among the Trobriands inhabiting parts of Vakuta Island (Papua New Guinea) was truly painful. Girls demonstrated their interest in boys by hurting them.

Special ceremonial gatherings took place for the purpose of selecting a sexual partner. At the beginning of the ceremony the boys walked around a public part of the village singing, while the girls teased the boys and cracked jokes about them.

Suddenly, however, the girls changed their attitude and each girl attacked a chosen boy with a sharp shell or a bamboo knife, making painful wounds. Boys accepted this torture as it was regarded as an act of invitation to sex. The girl who attacked the most vigorously was said to show best her own temperament as a future lover.

The beating and scratching by the girl were considered to be an expression of appreciation of the beauty of the chosen boy. A boy's ambition was to receive as many wounds as possible, since they signified how sexy he was.

Having suffered his scratches or wounds, the man took his reward on the same night by making love to his attacker. The intercourse might even be performed in a central place of the village as there was at that time complete licence in the Trobriand Islands.

For Trobriands sexual union had such a great ritual significance that it was even performed to commemorate the dead after funerals. When the mourners returned home after a burial ceremony some local girls had to remain in the house and make love to some of the boys in honour of the deceased person. The girl was forbidden to choose her usual lover.

2.
Becoming Sexy

Sexy Tattoo

In some cultures of the Pacific, it was customary for women to tattoo their sexual organs in the belief that it would make them more sexually attractive.

For this purpose the Ulithian women of the Western Pacific tattooed the inner lips of their vulvas. In some regions tattooing of genitals in women was included in their initiation rituals as the tattooing gave a girl the status of an adult woman. The tradition was so strong that in Nakuoro Island (South Pacific) if a child was born before a woman had been tattooed, the child had to be put to death.

Penis tattooing also occurs in some societies. Some men among the Mangaia (Cook Islands) even tattooed pictures of a vulva on their penis. Penis tattooing was not confined to commoners. One of the kings of Tonga had the entire glans of his penis covered with tattoos to demonstrate his total disregard for pain.

In Japan many prostitutes have distinctive tattoos to sexually excite their clients. These tattoos may be found on their breasts, inside their thighs and on their groin. A snake coiled about the woman's groin, and about to enter, is a common theme. Beautiful flowers can often be seen tattooed on a breast.

Tattooing as a body decoration is not solely confined to women practising the world's oldest profession; men belonging to the yakuza, the Japanese mafia, all have an elaborate tattoo since it signifies their belonging to the group.

There are about 110,000 yakuza members in Japan, and they are responsible for controlling everything from gambling and prostitution to 'protection' of various businesses. Yakuza men admire tattoos which may cover their whole body including penis. This is in fact a most delicate artistic achievement since the full details of the design on the penis, such as a peach or an egg-plant (both associated with sex), only become visible when the tattooed penis is erect. Tattooing is a costly and long operation as it may take 100 hours for an artist to decorate the entire body.

The reason the yakuza members tattoo their skin can be traced back to the remote past when there was a penalty of tattooing for those who committed a crime. The criminal would thus be visible to others in the community. A man convicted of robbery was forced to have a tattoo in the form of a cross on his forehead and a new tattoo was added for each additional crime. (When a criminal was brought to trial, his former convictions were already marked on his body.)

By tattooing, yakuza mark their members for ever. Tattoos are still so strongly linked with crime that a person who has a tattoo is not allowed to enter a public bath or sauna in Japan. This however does not cause any inconvenience for yakuza members since they have their own bath houses.

Tattoos are only one of the reasons why it is so difficult to leave the yakuza and this is not the most important one. The whole organisation is based on strict discipline and obedience. One yakuza leader admitted in the late 1980s: 'Disobedience or mistakes are punished by the ancient yakuza code of "enko zume", or shorten finger. Under the code a first offence is punished by cutting off the end joint of the little finger of the offender's left hand . . . if the person persists in his misguided ways, another joint, and even a third and fourth, may be removed.' While in the past the punishment had to be self-inflicted, nowadays this painful operation is carried out by someone else. Even now a significant number of yakuza members lack the end joint of the little finger.

It is worth mentioning that there are many enthusiasts of tattoo in the world. Some people collect tattoos made by the best artists. There are private galleries of tattooed skins in modern Japan. Some collectors make a deal for an attractive human skin before the owner is 'ready' to be skinned. Payments may be made in advance for the skin of the entire back of the tattooed person, although the buyer has to wait until the owner dies.

Vulva Contest

Truk Islanders were not only famous for their painful customs. Even more weird was their custom of extending a girl's vulva to make her more 'beautiful' and more sexually attractive. This was done by gradual elongation of the girl's labia minor. The longer the labia, the more sexually attractive a woman was as a love partner and with such an elongated vulva she had a much better chance of finding a handsome husband. Small wonder that mothers always reminded their daughters not to forget to pull their labia minor when they bathed.

It was also a common custom among Truk girls to improve nature in yet another way. They inserted tinkling objects into the pierced labia minor. Consequently, the objects sounded when the girl walked. This demonstrated her sexuality. The extended vagina and its tinkling was a matter of great honour to each local girl. If two girls began to quarrel and fight, one of the girls often undressed to challenge her opponent to a kind of a vulva contest. The girl who had the longer labia minor won. This unusual contest was even performed in the presence of men.

The custom of extending sexual organs in women was also known among certain tribes of South Africa. For example, Hottentot women used to greatly elongate the labia minor to protrude 'several inches beyond the vaginal entrance'. These women were proud of their unusual sexual lure which was called 'Hottentot apron'.

Erotic Foot

It seems incredible to consider a woman's foot a highly sexually stimulating organ. Yet, for over a thousand years, to Chinese men the especially deformed woman's foot was an erotic 'organ'.

The deformation was accomplished by binding the feet of very young girls. The process began at the age of five or six. The feet were bound with tight bandages so as to arrest their growth. As the girl grew older the bandages were tightened. Consequently, after several years the foot was reduced to a fraction of its natural size and it also considerably changed in appearance. Only the big toe remained unchanged. This was done in order to maintain balance when walking.

The forefoot and the heel were brought very close together, while the four lesser toes were curled under the sole. The deep cleft under the arch of the foot became fleshy and soft.

To Chinese men such a foot, called the lotus foot, was beautiful and graceful. In the soft cleavage under the arch of the deformed foot, they saw an equivalent of the female sexual organ. It was even customary among Chinese males to copy the female lotus foot by squeezing their own feet into very tight small shoes of the female type and to imitate elegant women's sensuous walk.

The lotus feet were said to be the property of a husband. Even close relatives were not allowed to touch them. Touching a lotus foot was considered to be an act of the most intimate nature. To a Chinese woman, the lotus foot represented her very personality and beauty. No wonder lotus feet were considered of particular value to women who were engaged in prostitution.

Although sexually attractive feet were most important in love-making it was not universal among ordinary people. However it was obligatory for aristocratic women. For them, lack of lotus feet was a serious obstacle to both courtship and marriage.

Even shoes had sexual connotations. In the Middle Ages in Europe there was a custom among males of wearing especially made shoes with turned-up toes, which had a phallus-like appearance. The elongated tip of the shoe, which could be up to 25 cm long, was stuffed with cork in order to keep it handsome and erect. To keep these extravagant decorations erect and to avoid tripping, a special chain was attached to the knee. Because of the attacks of the Church authorities on such an obvious indecency, the length of the tip was restricted to 15 cm for commoners, and a bit longer for noblemen. Some elegant men had the tips of their shoes in the colour and design of an erect penis and these extraordinary shoes were worn during decadent dinner parties in aristocratic circles.

Perfect Beauty

According to the Arabian Nights the ideal woman was 'to have breasts of white ivory, a harmonious belly, a glory of thighs, and buttocks like cushions'. In some societies these qualities were encouraged to the extreme. Travellers to Mauretania saw monstrously obese young girls who could hardly walk and had to be supported by two slaves. They learned with surprise that such girls were perfect beauties for whom there was great demand. All the local warriors 'vie for their favours'. According to local tradition the most beautiful was a girl who was no taller than 160 cm and whose weight was some 150 kg. Such a girl was sexually attractive because of her desirable oval shape, and because her skin was stretched by fat deposits she even had a lighter complexion.

To make their daughters more attractive to future husbands, the girls' mothers tried to make them obese before marriage. The young girls were forced to consume enormous amounts of nutritious dates and to drink up to five litres of milk every day. Mothers were so determined to make their girls look beautiful that they forced them to eat long after they had had enough. A mother would deliberately punch the girl's feet with a wooden stick to cause her to cry in pain. As she opened her mouth, the feeding mother would immediately stuff in more food.

A similar custom prevailed among the Tuareg girls of the Sahara. There, a girl's fatness was promoted by her family from an early age to make her more sexually attractive. The daughter of a rich family was entrusted to energetic slaves whose sole duty was to force her to swallow enormous quantities of starchy food and milk. To distribute the accumulated fat uniformly and to suppress angles, the girl was massaged vigorously and rolled in the sand. Due to such energetic efforts, towards the age of eighteen the girl was ideally monstrous. Such a beauty was often so heavy that she was unable to rise without the help of two strong slaves and when making a trip she was usually loaded on a camel because it was too difficult for her to walk.

On the other hand, among the Bushmen, to be beautiful a girl had to have her fat deposits located in one special part of her body; it was her enormously swollen buttocks which made the girl most sexually attractive.

By using a certain diet and special posture, the woman after some time accumulated so much fat in her buttocks that they appeared as extended as if they were a chair.

Such unusual corpulence was once thought in the West to represent a kind of human adaptation to the desert environment; it was even compared to the hump of a camel.

Fatness was also considered to be the most desirable quality among women of the Zapotec Indians of southern Mexico. To be slim would signify poor health and the best compliment for a woman was to say how fat and luxuriant she looked.

In many societies there has been great emphasis on the shape and size of women's breasts as a mark of beauty. Such widely separated people as the Hopi Indians of North America and the Thonga of East Africa were known to favour very large breasts.

The Azande of Central Africa on the other hand, wanted females to have pendulous breasts. Local girls tied special bands tightly across their bosom to force the breasts to hang down.

An opposite view about women's beauty was favoured in parts of Europe. In nineteenth-century Spain, the most beautiful were girls who had very small breasts. To achieve this ideal their breasts were covered with heavy leaden plates to prevent them from growing. Similarly, in Bavaria and Wurttemberg in Germany, wooden platters were attached firmly to girls' breasts to prevent their normal development. Consequently, the most 'beautiful' girls in this region had almost no breasts.

Men's Beauty Contest

Among the Fulani of West Africa it is not easy for a man to get married. To find a wife a young man must take part in a seven-day beauty contest during which he must be chosen by a girl. In order to become attractive the young man has to use the local cosmetics extensively. In fact, with all his decorations in place, to a Westerner the boy looks like an attractive woman. His lips are painted dark and his head is so decorated that he seems to have long hair. This is accomplished by hanging at each side of his face fringes of ram's beard, chains, beads and rings, while the hair is ornamented with beautiful ostrich feathers.

During the festival boys participating in the beauty contest stand in line, swaying gently and gracefully. To emphasise their beauty the boys roll their eyes and flash their teeth, showing their ideal whiteness.

But being nicely decorated and swaying gently is just not enough. There is as well a test of physical endurance in which a boy has to choose a challenger who will whip him. As Robert Brain explains: 'While he is beaten across his ochre-painted ribs, he expresses his virility and hence his sexuality by submitting without flinching, holding his arms above his head or languidly fingering a necklace while he gazes at his painted face in a mirror. Large weals result from this test and exhibition, and these are visible for life as raised ridges . . . these weals are highly prized as part of their body decoration'.

This demonstration of beauty and virility is carefully watched by the assembled young girls, while the old ladies make fun of those whom they consider ugly or not handsome enough. If a girl is sufficiently impressed by one of the boys she indicates her choice by advancing a few steps in front of the man. The happy chosen man follows the girl, who usually becomes his wife.

Fulani people are so obsessed with male beauty that the moment a boy is born his mother begins her efforts to make him beautiful. She applies a gentle pressure to the boy's head as if modelling it into a perfect sphere. As a straight long nose is regarded as one of the important attributes of male beauty, she tries to gently punch or press the child's nose into a fine shape. She may even pull the delicate limbs of the boy infant in the belief that he would be taller when he grows up. Although such efforts cannot have any actual effects on the boy's future appearance, they nevertheless show the aspirations of the mother to make her son a 'beautiful' man.

Human Giraffes

Women in Padaung, Burma are famous for the extraordinary decoration of their body. They wear brass rings around their necks and have their necks stretched up to 38 cm long. No wonder these women are called 'long necks' or 'giraffe-necked' women.

When a girl is about ten years old she is given five brass rings which she has to place around her neck. Year after year new rings are added. To make it possible for a woman to wear them she is subjected to many hours of neck manipulation and massage. Despite the pain involved, the girl remains patient since she knows that the more rings she wears the more sexually attractive she will be. An adult woman may have some twenty or more rings on her neck. They force her chin upwards and as a result her voice is described as strangulated. If a married woman committed adultery it was customary to punish her by removing all the rings from her neck. It was thought that such a 'wasted' neck would not be able to support the head and it would drop down. We now know that is not true. Many women who converted to Christianity had the rings removed from their necks and did not suffer any ill-effects.

Rings are put on to elongate the neck and are also placed as decoration on legs and arms. As these brass rings may be up to 0.8 cm thick, they are quite heavy. In the old days when a woman's body was decorated with many rings, it was a heavy price for beauty as the decorations could weigh some 30 kg.

Nobody knows why there is such an unusual requirement for beauty among the women in Padaung. One myth related to this custom says that in very remote times people in the region angered spirits which sent tigers to punish them. As a result of this invasion so many local women perished that there was a danger that no one would survive and this would mean the end of the tribe. During this crucial time their ancestors found a solution. They demanded that each woman protect her body from the tiger's attack by wearing brass armour. It was believed that even if a tiger attacked a woman, it would be unable to overpower her because of the hard brass rings on her neck.

Wearing rings as body decoration is also common in other regions of the world. The Makololo women of Malawi wear extraordinary plates which they insert in their upper lips. Called pelele, the lips are so distended that the person with them looks most unusual. Dr Livingstone, during his famous expedition in Africa, once asked the reason for this ornamentation. The answer of the chief was that it was of course for beauty, 'They are the only beautiful things women have. Men have beards, women have none. What kind of person would she be without the pelele? She would be not a woman at all'.

One of the most extravagant lip plates is used by the women of southern Chad. Although they are used to make women more attractive, such a decoration served the opposite aim in the past. It was believed that during the slave trade local girls used large lip discs to become ugly so that slave traders would ignore them and look for 'normal' looking girls.

Genital Sheath

An unusual type of modesty is practised by the Dani men of Irian Jaya. The local men do not cover their body except for their penis, which is constantly hidden under a sheath, although their testicles are uncovered. This peculiar decoration is held vertically by a fibrous string tied around the man's torso. The sheaths vary in size and shape and are often made of a gourd. Sometimes a chosen sheath has a twirl at the end so the owner looks especially handsome. Occasionally, men decorate the penis sheaths with a fur tuft to make them more attractive. As Philippe Diole wrote in 1976: 'Wamena, though hardly even a village, offers a unique spectacle unmatched by any of the great centres of the world. Everywhere

around the landing field, in the village's only store, under the trees—
groups of naked men were standing, their only attire a penile or
genital sheath. These sheaths, mostly golden yellow in colour, were
of every size and shape. Some were straight, others were curved,
and some were spiral. A few were so long that they touched the
wearer's chin and had to be held in place by a ribbon attached
to a belt'.

This peculiar custom exists even today, though the sheaths tend
to be shorter than in the past. Some Danis have modernised their
traditional sheaths by using such objects as empty cans or toothpaste
containers.

It is said that even those who now wear trousers like their old
custom so much that they have small penis covers under their
clothes.

In the past, penis sheaths were also common in Vanuatu. In some
areas the sheaths were made from leaves or bark cloth, in others
many metres of cotton were used to make a single sheath. Some
men preferred using horns, nuts or even shells as penis sheaths.
Often the sheaths were decorated with flowers or attractive animal
tails.

Although some Western travellers regard the penis sheaths as
characteristic of the most primitive societies, similar customs
existed in Europe. It became a fashion for an elegant man to attach
a pouch to the crotch of his tight-fitting breeches. Some of these
pouches, which were known as codpieces, had the qualities of
the penis sheaths. They were stuffed, decorated with embroidery
or bows and they often resembled an erect penis. Some codpieces
were so large that a man could use them to hide sweets, oranges
or a spoon. The custom of wearing codpieces was widespread in
Europe till the sixteenth century and survived in some regions
until the seventeenth century.

3.
The Most Bizarre Sexual Customs

Phallic Trophy

Until fairly recently the Danakils of Djibouti on the Red Sea were enthusiastic collectors of human phallic trophies. As recently as 1970, Professor I. M. Lewis reported: 'A warrior sports the genitals of his vanquished foes around his neck or decorates his tent with them'. Similar customs used to be practised by the Galla of Ethiopia. Among them, phallic trophies were of such value that no man could marry a girl until he provided her with this 'natural proof' of his manhood. Consequently, the local men became enthusiastic collectors of human phalli. To obtain the precious trophy, a warrior would either mutilate a prisoner of war or cut off the penis of a man killed by him in battle.

But phallic trophies were not only needed before marriage. To keep his marriage happy a man had to continue to confirm his manhood to his wife by supplying her with new phallic trophies. If he failed to do so his wife would live in shame as an outcast ridiculed by other wives.

In some regions of Africa real phallic trophies were later replaced by images of phalli. In one region of southern Ethiopia every adult man used to demonstrate his manhood by wearing a phallic effigy on his brow. It was made of light shining metal and it was regarded as a very important ritual emblem of an adult man. In fact it signified that the wearer had already killed an adult opponent.

In some regions of Ethiopia, however, this peculiar decoration was only allowed for priests of the highest rank or holders of special honours. In other words, it was an insignia of high rank. Even kings used to wear them.

In the past, the king of the great southern Ethiopian kingdom, Kaffa, was famous for the extraordinary three-part phallic effigy which he had on his brow. It was such a distinct emblem that it was even thought to be a strangely shaped royal crown.

In some regions of West Africa people used to worship phallic gods. As A. B. Ellis wrote in 1890: 'the phallus is seen everywhere, in front of houses, in the streets and public places, sometimes alone, but more frequently in connection with the image of Legba, to whom the organ is sacred, and whose principal attribute is the exciting of sexual desires'. He explained that both the Yoruba and Ewhe people 'attribute sexual desires to possession by the god' and that the god was believed to remove barrenness.

According to Geoffrey Parrinder, 'along the coast of Ghana many images outside towns had phallic appearance, with clay figures that had carefully shaped wooden phalli of exaggerated size, with bundles of similarly shaped wooden rods laid in front of them'. In Porto Novo the capital of Benin (formerly Dahomey) Parrinder saw on a main road . . . 'a life-sized clay figure of a European, wearing a sun helmet and wristwatch and with a big phallus'.

Writing in 1912, P. A. Talbot tells us that among the Ekoi of Nigeria a medicine was produced to propitiate the deity responsible for plentiful harvest. The main constituent of the medicine was a human sexual organ, preferably that of a woman. For this purpose every year a human was killed and the organ removed. Among certain people of Cameroon only males were sacrificed.

Bizarre Phallus

Some races who were impressed by the sexual behaviour of certain animals tried to mutilate their sexual organs so that they would resemble those of a beast, in the belief that this would enhance their own sexual abilities. In some regions of Borneo people noticed that the Sumatran rhino can copulate for about one hour, so they decided to imitate the rhino's penis. They noticed that the rhino's penis has two strange sausage-like flanges about 5 cm long, which dangle from the penis shaft like a crossbar on both sides of the sexual organ. Trying to resemble the rhino, they inserted pieces of bamboo into their penises.

On the other hand, in Australia, some Aborigines have been

impressed by the sexual behaviour of kangaroos. They claim that the animals can copulate for up to two hours. Small wonder then that they want their penises to resemble those of a kangaroo. The kangaroo penis is two-headed (bifid) and the adult men in some Aboriginal societies mutilate their penises to look the same. As a result they are unable to direct the flow of their urine and have to squat to urinate. This peculiar practice was most common among the Aborigines living in central and northwestern Australia.

Penis-holding Rite

In most societies hand-shaking is regarded as the symbol of peace. But among some Australian Aborigines, it was the rite of penis-holding which was a sign of peace, indicating also the settling of a dispute or cessation of a hostility. This strange custom existed as late as 1945 among some groups of Bidjandjara at Mucumba in north-eastern Australia.

At a certain period following male circumcision, it was customary for every male stranger who entered the camp to perform the penis-holding ritual with other men. As Ronald and Catherine Berndt reported: 'Women and children at once covered their heads and shoulders to avoid witnessing this secret rite. Bending before each man in turn the visitor would take hold of the other's arms and place his penis in the palm of the other's hand . . . then the visitor would sit down while the other men did the same to him.' When the rite was completed, the women and children uncovered their eyes and everything returned to normal.

The rite of penis-holding played an essential role in settling disputes and could be used if a man accused of some misdeed wanted to clear himself. In such a case a special meeting was arranged during which the accused person sat with a group of his male friends, while the accusing man sat with his. Then the head man of the latter group stood up and performed the penis-holding greeting with everyone present while ignoring the suspected man. Then the suspect tried to defend himself while his friends supported his stand by claiming that the accusation was false.

Once the accuser decided to drop his charge, everybody approached both the defender and the accused and performed the penis-holding ritual with them. Later the accused man would perform the penis-holding gesture with one of his most eloquent defenders, thanking him in this manner for saving his life.

If the accused man would not wait for the verdict but ran away during the meeting, his action was viewed as the admission of guilt. The members of the opponent group would throw spears at him, often killing him on the spot.

If the accused was not a man but a woman, her male relatives could stand in for her at the meeting. Sometimes though the accused woman decided to attend such a meeting herself. She usually arrived with a group of her male supporters who declared that they were there to defend her. After patiently listening to her accusers, she would tell them that she wanted to meet them alone somewhere outside the camp. If the accusers followed the woman into a secluded place she 'gave herself up' to each man. Accepting such an invitation to intercourse was regarded as having the same power as the penis-holding rite. If no one rejected her offer the whole matter was closed. Should any of the accusing men refuse her offer another meeting had to be arranged.

Genital Padlocks

In Europe, in order to guarantee the chastity of women, a bizarre invention called the 'chastity belt', a kind of metal frame, was fastened with a padlock and attached about the waist and pelvis of a woman in such a way that sexual intercourse was impossible. The belt had only a small opening to enable the woman to perform the necessary functions. Some chastity belts were more 'sophisticated' in that they had barbed openings.

Chastity belts originated in Europe during the late Middle Ages. It was believed that the crusaders fastened chastity belts to their wives before leaving home for the Holy Land, but this claim has not been confirmed. It is certain, however, that during the crusades, one of the German emperors ordered a blacksmith to rivet an iron frame on his wife which was removed only when he returned from the campaign against the Saracens.

This peculiar practice was mainly confined to France and Italy, where original chastity girdles can be seen in many museums. As Voltaire once said: '. . . to guard the virtue of his woman a gentleman lays up a stock of girdles and padlocks. There, every jealous man, without fear or blame, holds under lock and key the virtue of his dame'.

The chastity belts were in such great demand that special dealers offered them in city markets. In one case in medieval France, five noblemen purchased chastity belts for their wives from a local blacksmith.

They later discovered that their wives still accepted lovers in their absence. The angry customers accused the blacksmith of making extra profits by selling duplicate keys to other interested gentlemen of the town. Some men in medieval Austria kept their 'sexual property' locked in a chastity belt even after death. In 1889 the skeleton of a woman was excavated in which the pelvic region was encircled by a metal chastity belt, secured by locks.

Despite the fact that the use of chastity belts has long been forgotten, according to some reports there are still small factories in some parts of Europe which produce such devices for jealous husbands.

Similar chastity devices were also common in the Near East. When a husband decided to permit his wife to visit her friend and there was no slave eunuch to accompany her, the husband fastened a 'chastity' device of an iron or leather band with a hole in front of the vulva, through which a round wooden stick was inserted into the vagina. It was inserted in such a way that only the woman's husband could remove it.

This custom was also known among Plains Indians such as the Cheyenne. Their girls had to wear an easily removable chastity belt until marriage and after marriage when their husbands were away. Special chastity corsets were also used by women of certain tribes in the Caucasus. Not surprisingly, all these inventions appear to have developed independently of each other.

Polluting Sex

Some people in Africa still believe that sexual intercourse has a polluting effect on those who engage in it. Furthermore, it is not just the sexual partners themselves who become polluted but they can also pollute other 'innocent' people just by standing in close proximity to them. This is the case among the Bechuana people of Southern Africa, where a person who has recently had sex is urged not to visit ill people as the polluting effect of his visit would be so strong that the sick person might not recover.

The most dangerous polluting effect is said to occur when the sick person hears the voice of a person who has recently engaged in sex. For this reason those who care for the sick person must refrain from sex until he or she recovers.

Fear of pollution by sex is so strong that special purification rites are performed after each sexual act. There is also a strange custom of purification of all the people of the community at the beginning of each year to remove the pollution caused by sexual unions.

Another purification ceremony is required for all those married women who committed adultery during the preceding year. It is a rather peculiar rite performed by the priest in the presence of both partners. The guilty woman has to sit on the ground during this rite opposite her husband, so close that her knees are between his own. A pot containing a burning herb is placed between the man's knees for ritual purification by fumigation. Then the 'merciful' husband makes a small cut on the skin under the navel of the unfaithful wife and she makes a similar cut on the man's abdomen. The blood obtained from these incisions is collected, mixed with certain herbal potions and then rubbed into the incisions of both participants. This is the end of the peculiar purifying rite and the couple return home.

Vulva Thief

The strangest attitude of husbands towards their wives could be observed in the past among the Maritime Koryaks of Siberia. Among these people the husband felt most honoured when his wife engaged in a sexual union with a stranger. For this reason the Koryak men used to offer their wives for sexual pleasure to any stranger who happened to be passing by. During Tsarist times in Russia travellers, and especially postmen, were being literally begged by the married men to sleep with their wives.

Once when a guest returned to the same place after a year or so he received extraordinary treatment. The husband was so happy to meet him again that he offered him numerous precious gifts. The reason for his unusual joy was that a boy was born as a result of a previous sexual union between the stranger and the host's wife.

It is therefore rather surprising to learn that other Koryaks had an entirely different attitude towards sexual relations. Among those people sexual hospitality was unthinkable and a husband who discovered that his wife had illicit sexual intercourse would immediately kill both partners. The jealousy of married men in those regions was so great that wives tried to prevent hostility by making themselves as unattractive to other men as possible.

Consequently, when outside her house a woman used to wear dirty and torn clothing, and even covered herself with rags so that no one would look at her with desire.

Sexual hospitality was customary in some regions of Siberia and was common in the old days in Tibet. As Marco Polo reported with surprise when he visited Tibet in the thirteenth century: 'No man considers himself wronged if a foreigner or any other man, dishonours his wife or daughter, or any woman in the family. On the contrary, he deems such intercourse a piece of good fortune. And they say that it brings the favour of their gods and idols, and great increase of temporal prosperity. For this reason they bestow their wives on foreigners and other people'.

Among some Eskimos there was a custom of lending wives for short periods. Such a wife was allowed to take part in a hunting expedition with a man who was not her husband and during this time she became his sexual partner and cook. This arrangement was usually made among the members of the same clan as they were regarded as bond-brothers. It was also customary that if such a bond-brother who lived in another village paid a visit to his brother's house he could share his wife.

Interestingly the custom of lending wives for sexual pleasure was also known in medieval Europe. In Ireland such sexual hospitality was the privilege of the mighty king of the country or his sons. When Aed MacAinmarch, the son of the king of Ireland was travelling in the country, each night he was given a new girl for his pleasure. It was also customary that even an ordinary traveller was offered a woman for sexual pleasure when he had to stay at a given house for the night. If the host did not want to offer his own wife to a guest, he could bestow his female relatives or a servant as a substitute.

Sexual hospitality was once a common custom in Japan. It survived in some regions of Japan until the Middle Ages, but the custom involved only women who were the wives of some bureaucrats. When a high-ranking official was dispatched to a distant province of Japan, the wife of the resident lower rank official was obliged to fulfil his sexual needs. If she refused to become a 'wife for the night' as the custom was called, her husband was punished by immediate dismissal from his post.

Among certain tribes of Australian Aborigines (e.g. Arunta), a husband had the right to transfer sexual rights over his wife to another man for a temporary period, provided both men belonged to the same special group. Throughout this time the husband was the master of his wife in the sense that he could withhold his consent at any time. If, however, someone had sex with his wife without the permission of the husband, he was regarded as a criminal and was called a vulva-thief.

Incredible Defloration Rituals

It was the custom in some societies that a girl had to lose her virginity before she attained puberty. Among the Todas living in southern India a young girl had to be deflowered by a stranger. It was such an important event that if the expected deflowering was not carried out or delayed, the girl lived the remainder of her life in disgrace and no man would marry her. To avoid this the girl's parents would invite a young man, usually from another clan, to spend a night in the girl's family house. The guest's duty was to have sexual intercourse with the young virgin girl.

A similar custom prevailed in some regions of the Philippines where there were men who specialised in this defloration by request. This was in fact the source of their livelihood.

In some regions of the world defloration of girls was even performed in public. For example, on the Marquesas Islands (French Polynesia) defloration was the privilege of the oldest man in the village. It was a rather unusual event. According to a report by L. Lautain written in the mid nineteenth century, such a public defloration was carried out in the following way: 'On a signal from the husband all the men present join together to form a file, singing and dancing, and each in turn copulates with the bride, who is laying in a corner on a platform of stones with her head between the husband's knees. The procession which began with the oldest . . . finishes with the great chiefs, and last of all the husband'.

In Peru at the time of the Spanish conquest, it was customary for each girl to be deflowered just before her marriage. But it was not a stranger who was invited to do so but the girl's mother. It was a public event. The mother broke the hymen of her daughter while a crowd watched. The mother was very proud as she could demonstrate the girl's value to a potential husband.

In some European countries deflowering girls before marriage was the privilege of noblemen or even kings. The book of Leinster which dates from the middle of the twelfth century, describes the peculiar custom then prevailing in Ireland. The book states that Conchobar, the king of Ulster, slept with all the girls in his kingdom who patiently awaited their turn.

Similar customs were once common in other parts of Europe. Up to the time of the French Revolution, the king of France had the right, guaranteed by law, to sleep with every maiden on the first night after her marriage. This unusual custom known as 'jus primae noctis' (the right to the first night) was so notorious that abolishing it is said to have become one of the causes of the French Revolution. Of course the French king could not exert his right to every virgin girl of his kingdom, so it was customary for him to delegate this authority to other noblemen. The wife, however, could escape from 'jus primae noctis' if her husband was rich enough to pay a substantial amount of money to the noble who held the right delegated by the king.

Twenty Tokens

In Babylon and certain other places, every girl had to have sex before she was deemed good for marriage. Hence, a virgin could not marry. In Marco Polo's Tibet even this requirement was regarded as inadequate. There, a girl had to have sex with at least twenty strangers who accepted her of their own free will. The greater the number of men with whom she slept the better, since it showed how attractive she was.

The reader may well ask how she could prove to her prospective husband that she really had sex with a given number of men. The answer is simple. As Marco Polo explained 'Every lover was supposed to give her a ring or some other trifle, something in fact that she can show as a lover's token when she comes to be married'.

In Tibet old women had to work hard to help young ones in their endeavour to find lovers, since collecting the required number of tokens was not easy. Whenever travellers came to the village, mothers or female relatives approached them and offered the girls to whoever was willing. After making love the girls were returned to the old women since 'they are not allowed to follow the strangers away from home'. Consequently, travelling men, when they reached a village could have sex with about twenty or thirty girls.

The Son of an Uncut Mother

Although most people are familiar with circumcision in males, it seems incredible to claim that similar operations have been performed on women. Yet such operations take place even today. The most widespread female circumcision, known as clitori-dectomy, involves removal of the clitoris. This cruel custom is still quite common in many parts of Africa. In Europe this operation used to be practised as a cure for 'excessive' masturbation.

In Africa this painful operation is believed to make a woman clean and more sexually attractive. In some regions it is a serious insult for a man to be called the 'son of an uncut mother'. It is believed that clitoridectomy is very important because the clitoris is the woman's most sexually aggressive part, causing women to exhibit an unnatural appetite for sexual intercourse.

Some peoples of Eastern Africa remove not only the clitoris but also the labia minor. This operation, called infibulation, is carried out in such a way that the vagina is then sewn up, making sexual intercourse impossible. This operation is still performed among certain tribes in Sudan on small girls aged between five and seven. The girl is treated during this ritual circumcision as if she were a bride. She is beautifully dressed and adorned with golden ornaments, and her hands and feet are painted with henna.

A Mr F. Paney witnessed this event in Sudan. He wrote: 'When the hour comes, the child is laid on a bed and held down in position by the assembled women, while the matron, kneeling between the patient's thighs, begins by slicing off the tip of the clitoris and the edges of the inner lips, then the razor shears along the rims of the outer lips, removing a ribbon of flesh about two inches wide'.

As no anaesthetic is employed it is an extremely painful operation and the girl shrieks in pain. It is customary for the assembled friends witnessing the operation to make the loudest possible noise to deafen the cries of the suffering girl. When the operation, which takes four to five minutes is over, the assisting women express their great delight by saying that the girl has now become a real woman. They proudly repeat various slogans having sexual connotations such as, 'bring her a penis', 'she is ready for intercourse.'

With a deep incision made during such an operation a scar is finally formed after healing and this scar closes the vulva almost completely. Only a small orifice is left into which a hollow reed tube is usually inserted to enable passing of water and menstruation.

Infibulation is said to be an ideal means of safeguarding the girl's virginity before marriage. But when the circumcised girl reaches the age of marriage another operation is performed in order to make sexual intercourse possible. It takes place after the wedding ceremony, when an expert matron makes a longitudinal slash, and then inserts a wooden cylinder of a proper size to extend the vagina. This cylinder remains there for about two weeks until the wound has healed. Surprisingly, among some tribes of the region a wooden model of the penis is inserted into the vagina instead of a wooden cylinder.

Similar practices were common among the Conibo of Peru who inserted into the girl's mutilated vagina a clay dildoe which was an exact replica of her fiance's penis.

Ritual Intercourse

There was a weird custom among the Tsonga tribes of Southern Africa which related to the founding of a new village. These people lived in communities consisting of a head man, his wives and children and the wives and children of their married sons. The site of the new settlement was always chosen by the head man. When this was decided, a special ritual had to be performed at the chosen place. Ritual sexual intercourse of the most important community members, that is of a head man and his principal wife, took place in the evening. Next morning a special grass knot was made over which all the family members were obliged to step.

From this point on a strict taboo on sexual intercourse was observed by all community members. It lasted about a month, until the new village huts were all constructed. Strangely, it was believed that breaking the sexual taboo during this period would endanger not the guilty party but the health of the village head man. It was customary for the men who were busy transferring their huts to the new location to avoid any help from women and to show their hostile attitude by singing obscene songs insulting the women. The women's job was to smear the hut floors with mud and during this they retaliated by singing obscene songs ridiculing their men. They explained this unusual behaviour by saying that because the old village was destroyed, normal laws and decency had also to be broken for a specified period of time.

But when the huts were in their new places and the fence

surrounding the new village had been made, another sexual ritual was required. All the couples of the new settlement had to have sex. It had to be done in a fixed order of precedence; each principal wife would be the last to sleep with her husband. Once this second sexual rite was over, the head man's principal wife made offerings to ancestral spirits, begging them for their blessings on the new village.

Religious Castration

In the past, castration of people was sometimes practised for religious reasons. Since the sexual organs were regarded as the most precious possession of the male, they were regarded as the most worthy sacrifice to the gods. Especially demanding were the fertility goddess Cybele of the ancient Greeks, and the Syrian goddess Astarte of Hierapolis. These goddesses had to be served in their temples only by castrated priests.

The eunuch priests exhibited their remarkable devotion to the goddess Astarte especially during the annual religious festival when thousands of pilgrims arrived. When the colourful celebration in the street was taking place, the eunuch priests slashed themselves with knives. The sight of blood and the devotion of priests made such an impact on some worshippers that they decided to castrate themselves in public. As Sir James Frazer reported: 'A man flung his garments from him, leaped forth with a shout, and seized one of the swords which stood ready for the purpose, castrated himself on the spot. Then he ran through the city, holding the bloody pieces in his hand, till he threw them into one of the houses which he passed in his mad career'. The devotee was immediately given a female dress, and female ornaments, which he then had to wear till the end of his life. Similar sacrifices of human virility were made in honour of the fertility goddess Cybele in ancient Greece during a celebration known as the Day of Blood.

In ancient Egypt piles of freshly severed parts could be seen beneath the altars, where young men castrated themselves during initiation ceremonies. As late as 1896, J. R. Farnell reported the occurrence of religious castration among the Ba-Bwende and Ba-Sundi of Zaire.

Eunuchs played a very important role in some regions in the past; in China they were often given high positions. Some even became generals in the army or king's advisers. In Persia, some eunuchs became shahs, the main reason for their appointment being the fact that they did not have children so there was no rivalry after they died.

There was a custom in imperial China that the castrated parts of a eunuch were kept in a special container till the end of his life and buried with him. The amputated parts were put through a kind of pickling process to preserve them for many years. These amputated organs were occasionally used by a eunuch as a kind of certificate when he was looking for a job.

Although the Koran forbids castration, eunuchs played an important role in many Islamic houses. They were almost ideal for harems where ordinary male servants were forbidden. Producing eunuchs for harems became a great business in Arabic countries and it was the Christians who castrated the men and sold them for the demanding market.

Interestingly, there was a particular kind of eunuch called elghazee. Their testicles were cut off but the penis remained and did not lose its erectile power. Such eunuchs were very popular among the women in harems and became passionate lovers. Some became virtual rulers of harems. One such eunuch said: 'In everything God hath created for man there is use. For He to Whom be glory made the hands to seize, the feet to walk, the eyes to see, the ears to hear, and the penis to increase and multiply and so on with all the members of the body except the two bollocks. There is no use in them. So, one day, a slaver took out his knife and cut mine off, and ever since then, I have enjoyed thousands of women—and not a one have I sown with child'. For a woman sexual intercourse with a eunuch was most satisfying because such a lover had the 'charming ability to copulate almost indefinitely'.

Among the Hottentots of South Africa it was believed that a man must remove one of his testicles in order to prevent the birth of twins, as twins were considered bad luck to the family. Removal of one of the testicles was also customary among the inhabitants of the Caroline Islands (Micronesia) where young boys of about sixteen years old were ritually semi-castrated. The remaining testicle could also occasionally be cut off as a demonstration of loyalty to a chief, especially during war.

4.
Sexual Rituals in Japan

Phallic Deities

A number of fascinating fertility festivals in Japan still survive. The behaviour of men during such festivals is truly incredible. Masked, and dressed in outlandish carnival costumes, they demonstrate their virility with out-sized papier-mâché penises. Using the artificial phalli they 'chase' women in the street and prod them with these paper 'organs'. In some fertility festivals the men enter houses to find women to touch with the artificial phalli. (The phalli used to be made of wood.)

During some fertility celebrations phallic effigies are carried in procession along the street on small shrines. Sometimes in these parades a monstrous phallus is carried. One incredible effigy is displayed during the annual fertility festival in Nagano; this truly giant stone phallus weighs over two tons and is carried along the street by 100 men.

Kawasaki near Tokyo is famous for its unusual temple containing huge iron phalli. The temple is known as the Metal Phallus Deity Shrine and it is devoted to a phallic deity called Kanamara-sama. In this temple there are two iron phalli set on wooden frames; they resemble big cannons.

Barren women from all over Japan come to this temple in the belief that by praying to the fertility deity they will conceive. Among the many pilgrims who arrive there are parents whose wish has already been fulfilled. They bring their babies to place them in gratitude on the phallic effigy.

The temple is especially busy during the annual fertility festival. Children lick phallic lollipops and eat bananas topped with a circular blob of pink chocolate. Even toys sold during this ceremony are made in the shape of phalluses.

The Tagata shrine has the largest collection in Japan of erotic talismans. They are mostly phallic symbols. The objects have all been donated by grateful parents whose children were conceived under the influence of a sacred tree growing in the shrine's garden. Tourists can see the phallic objects during an annual procession of the shrine's treasures which takes place every 15 March. During the ceremony visitors can see many women holding wooden phalluses.

There are a number of phallic deities in Japan called Dosojin. They are the guardians of roads and village boundaries. They are worshipped in the form of stone images along the roadsides. The statues are round or phallic in shape and a few feet in height. As Oto Tokihiko wrote in 1983, thousands of them can be seen in the countryside. Dosojin can also be shown as a loving couple holding hands or in coitus in a stone relief which may also have a phallic shape. According to George Elder 'the god's rites, at New Year, are lively to the point of licence: bands of mischievous youths are allowed to roam, good-natured insults are exchanged, and Dosojin's own image may be beaten or urinated upon'.

Japanese Vagina Festival

Every year in Japan, in the city of Inuyama, near Nagoya, a very strange celebration known as the Vagina Festival takes place. It is celebrated on 15 March at the Ogata shrine. There is a great parade in which the most conspicuous object is a huge model of a clamshell which represents the vagina symbol of a female deity. The clam opens and closes as it is carried through the street; a small girl seated inside the pink of the clam throws out rice cakes to the watching crowd. An important part of this weird carnival is a display of various vulvar-phallic themes.

Worship of the vagina is believed to ensure marital harmony as well as helping unmarried people to find a good partner for marriage. It was believed that the deity in honour of which the festival was held had the power to cure venereal diseases. In the past, the vulva was not only considered to have fertility power but was believed to be able to repel demons.

Every five years, there is a ceremony in which the effigies of both male and female sexual organs are displayed. It is held in

Inuyama. This time the phallic objects are brought from the nearby Tagata shrine while the effigies of vulva are obtained from Ogata shrine.

During the many phallic festivals held in Japan, the sexual act itself is sometimes displayed. For example, at the end of the great phallic festival at Chiba, near Tokyo, a giant wooden phallus is inserted into a giant straw effigy of a vulva. To further symbolise the fertility act, the spectators spatter the effigy of the female organ with milk-like raw sake called doboroku.

5.

Sex and Initiation

Men's 'Menstruation'

The inhabitants of Wogeo Island off the coast of New Guinea have a truly extraordinary initiation to adulthood for their boys. The first stage of the initiation takes place when the boys are very young, usually just five years old. The adult men of the village make a surprise attack on the hut in which the boy lives and take him away from his weeping mother. The boy is led to the darkest area of the forest where his ears are pierced while the men shout at him and bang to frighten him. He is then told a terrifying story about a horrible, man-eating monster in the forest who has already detected the boy's presence and will soon arrive to devour him. This, of course, does not happen and the frightened boy is soon taken back to his mother's hut.

The second stage of the initiation takes place a number of years later. The boy is once again captured by the village men who take him to the men's communal house. The boy's treatment is extremely harsh there. Instead of his normally tasty food he receives the most unpleasant meals the men can think of, for example bitter roots. In an effort to make his stay more unpleasant, the boy is frequently beaten. Then, one day, at dawn, the boy is dragged by a strong adult man from the communal house to a sacred place at the beach, where the assembled men once again frighten the boy by telling him that the monster's attack is now imminent and that he will soon die a horrific death. Then the terrified boy is told a completely different story, namely that he will not be devoured by the monster but that in order to pass the next stage of the initiation he must learn how to play the sacred flute which is then given to him.

He has to promise that he will not tell anybody, especially his mother, about the existence of the sacred flute. Through this promise the boy transfers his loyalty from his mother to the adult men with whom he will now live till his marriage.

This is not the end of his initiation; although he is to play the sacred flute he cannot because his tongue is polluted. The men say that the boy's tongue is unclean because he sucked his mother's breast as a baby. He must first undergo a very painful purification ritual. It involves scraping his tongue with the rough leaf of a sandpaper tree. Profuse bleeding of the boy's tongue is regarded as an efficient act of purification. The initiate then starts learning to play the sacred flute and enters adulthood.

Although no more tongue-bleeding is required after this single purification, blood-letting continues to be common among the adult males. Their obsession with purity is so strong that they believe they become polluted after sexual intercourse with their wives, and that more 'cleansing', must be done by blood-letting. And this blood-letting is performed by making an incision in the penis. This ritual cleansing causes such profuse bleeding that it is often called 'men's menstruation'.

Blood-letting is so important a method of purification that even funerals or construction of new houses all require purification in the form of blood-letting from various parts of the body.

Extraordinary Punishment

Some of the most incredible attitudes towards sexual intercourse are held by the Kagaba people of northern Colombia. Their attitude towards incest is extraordinary; although incest is considered a horrific act and their religion strictly forbids it, their penalty for it is that the guilty pair must repeat the sinister act.

The logic of such an unusual stand hinges on the Kagaba belief that incest insults the spirit of sexuality called Heisei, a very revengeful spirit. To avoid his anger the spirit has to be appeased by the ritual of performing the same act again. Even when brother-sister or father-child, they must repeat the offensive act but differing from the original sexual intercourse in that all the ejaculated semen must be collected, wrapped in a special cloth and then handed to a priest who makes an offering to the spirit of sexuality to ensure his forgiveness.

This extraordinary punishment for incest is truly amazing. Is there anywhere a penalty for a crime which involves repeating the same crime? Such a penalty is not 'painful', and this is probably the reason why incest remains so common among the Kagabas.

Surprisingly, most Kagaba men hate having sex, although they normally marry. The reason for such a peculiar stand arises from the male's first sexual experience long before marriage. It is customary among the Kagabas that at initiation to adulthood a boy must have his first sexual intercourse with an ugly, toothless and very old woman. Small wonder that he would remember this love-making as the most unpleasant experience of his life. For this reason, it is said most Kagaba men do not enjoy sexual intercourse. Sex, even when they marry a woman of their choice, remains an undesirable affair.

Some anthropologists argue, however, that their lack of interest in sex is the result of their extensive chewing of coca leaves. In high doses coca substantially decreases male sexual drive. Unusually, the Kagaba men seem not to be ashamed of their evident handicap, as they freely talk about their hatred of sexual intercourse and even seem to be proud of it.

Small wonder that with such an attitude from their husbands, the Kagaba married women are most unhappy wives. They are even known to attack their men and 'rape' them in order to satisfy their sexual desires. It is the only society in the world in which women organise gangs to sexually assault males.

But this is not the end of surprises among the Kagabas. They have another peculiar custom, this time related to human semen. During intercourse, they say human semen must not fall on the earth because it would offend the gods who in their anger may totally destroy the whole universe. To prevent the dangerous waste of semen, special stones are placed beneath the male sexual organ during intercourse to catch any seminal flow.

Ceremonial Burial

Unlike other Indian societies, among the Cuna Indians of Panama it is not the boys but the girls who must undergo a painful initiation to adulthood before they can engage in sex. The first rite takes place at the onset of the girl's first menstruation. For the rite, a special hut is constructed from plantain leaves. The hut has no roof. The girl in the hut then has cold water poured over her. This 'watering' is performed by two girls especially appointed for the task, but the duration of the cold shower is almost impossible to grasp as true. It continues for four days. The girls pouring the water show no compassion for the girl in the hut, who shivers from extreme cold.

When the ritual is nearly over, fruits are brought from the forest, indicating that the girl can free herself. She quickly destroys the hut and gets out of her symbolic prison. She then paints her body with the fruit juice. After her decorations of her body are completed she returns home.

The first initiation is insufficient though. The girl must undergo a second rite which is so painful that the first one looks like pleasure. The second ritual is most peculiar as it involves a ceremonial burial. The girl is buried up to her shoulders in the ground during a special gathering led by a local shaman. When the shaman begins his ritual chanting his assistant takes pieces of hot amber and starts to burn the girl's hair, attaching the amber to various parts of her head. The girl suffers great pain which is only occasionally relieved by cold water poured over her head. This unusual ordeal takes some six hours. When the girl is finally picked up from her 'half-grave' she is so weak that she looks as though she is about to die. She is unable to stand and she is carried away to a hammock to recuperate from her ordeal. But interest in the girl by spectators ceases completely. They begin to dance joyfully and the celebration continues until everybody is exhausted.

It is worth mentioning that the Cunas' cold-water shower used to initiate their girls is also applied to new-born babies. The custom is that an expecting mother is laid in a hammock with a big hole in the middle. Through this hole the newborn baby falls straight down into a canoe filled with water which is positioned beneath the hammock. Although this first shower must be very unpleasant for the baby, it is believed that this makes it immune to ill-health.

Initiation with a Skull

For the Asmats of Irian Jaya a human skull was absolutely essential during their initiation rituals. At the beginning of the ceremony a specially decorated skull was placed between the legs of the initiate who sat naked on the floor of the ceremonial hut. He was obliged to press the skull against his genitals and stare at it constantly for up to three days. In this way it was believed the initiate would absorb the total sexual power of the skull owner. This was the ticket to his sexual maturation.

When the first ritual was over, the candidate was led to the sea, where a canoe was waiting for him. The initiate had to stand in the canoe as it sailed and the ceremonial skull was placed in front of him. The canoe sailed in the direction of the sun, where it was believed the people's ancestors lived. During this journey, accompanied by his uncle or an adult relative, the initiate had to play several roles. He had first to behave as if he were an old man, so weak that he could not stand any more, falling to the canoe floor. The accompanying man then lifted him and immersed him and the skull in the sea. This act symbolised the death of the old man and it was said that a new man was reborn.

Accordingly, the candidate then had to play the role of a baby, unable to walk, or talk. He had to show that he was gradually growing up and learning these things from his elder relative. When the canoe finally returned to shore, the initiate had to behave like an adult man. And from now on he had to adopt the name of the skull owner as his own.

This is why for the Asmats, who were notorious head hunters, it was so important to know the name of a person they killed. A head whose name remained unknown was useless as it could not be used in their initiation ceremonies.

The Asmats' passion for human heads was first described by the Reverend Gerald Zegward who was the first white man to live for several years among them. He was lucky to stay alive. He was not decapitated because he was captured while asleep and the cannibals could not kill him without first learning his name. By withholding this information from his captors, the clever pastor survived and even became a good friend to them.

In 1954 the pastor described the following interesting case. Three strangers were guests of one of the Asmat village men who had invited them to a party. Although the Asmats were very hospitable, they of course looked at the guests as a source of skulls and planned their decapitation during the meeting. A special song was first sung to honour them and then the guests were asked their names, being told that the Asmats wanted to include them in their traditional song. Once the Asmats learned their guests' names they immediately decapitated them.

The Asmats' obsession with human heads and their custom of decapitation is believed to have originated from their observation of the strange behaviour of a praying mantis; the Asmats were impressed by the female mantis who normally bites off the male's head during copulation.

Asmats did not only practise head-hunting to get skulls for initiation. Human brains were considered a delicacy. It was also customary to remove the lower jaw of the enemy's skull and hang it around the warrior's neck as a decoration and trophy.

The Asmats regarded the skulls of their ancestors as most precious objects. These skulls were beautifully polished and were used by warriors as pillows in the belief that placing their heads on these skulls enabled them to absorb the strength and bravery of their ancestors.

Magic Teeth

Among certain Australian Aboriginal tribes no young man could enjoy sex unless he had sacrificed one of his teeth; one or more of a boy's front teeth were simply knocked out at his initiation ceremony.

The teeth were not simply discarded. Among some tribes of the region on the Darling River (New South Wales) the initiate's extracted tooth had to be placed under the bark of a chosen tree and then the tooth's fate was carefully observed. If it was later found that bark had covered the hidden tooth, it was a good omen. But if the tooth had become exposed and covered in ants, it was concluded that the tooth's owner would suffer from a serious disease.

Among some tribes in New South Wales it was customary that a tooth from a novice became the property of an elder of the tribe. The tooth was later given to another community member, so that the tooth 'travelled' around the whole community, finally being returned to the tooth owner himself. It was believed that during its 'travels' the tooth could counter dangerous magic which might endanger the life of the initiated man.

A white traveller who was present at one initiation ceremony was given the privilege of carrying the teeth of some initiates after extraction. The visitor was surprised when after about a year an elderly man travelled a hundred miles to visit him in order to retrieve one of the teeth. One of the initiates had become seriously ill and it was concluded that his tooth had been influenced magically and caused the boy's illness.

On Alor Island, Indonesia, tooth shape and colour are of particular importance. The custom was that adolescents of both sexes had to beautify their teeth by blackening, shortening and making them even.

The procedure was lengthy, and was performed by a professional tooth blackener. It was still being done in the 1940s. A special paste made of black earth and other plant ingredients was smeared on a strip of bark and cut to fit the mouth of the girl or boy. The bark was placed inside the mouth against the teeth and attached in position by flexible strips of bark. For up to ten days the youngster kept this in his mouth and was fed with small pieces of food. Long bamboo tubes were used for drinking.

After the blackening was finished, the same specialist performed a second, rather unpleasant operation which lasted two to three hours. The mouth of the boy or girl was jammed open with a corncob. Then, six upper and six lower teeth were filed down to half their length. The teeth were filed down to a straight, even line and were considered to look attractive, especially when smiling. Tooth blackening and shortening were regarded as preliminaries to marriage for young people.

School of Love

Although initiation of males to adulthood often involves pain, it does not normally include sexual training. However, in Vanuatu, sexual training was an essential part of a boy's initiation.

Before the initiation ritual all young males lived together in a special house; a woman called Iowhanan was invited into this house to teach the young men the secrets of making love. Her instructions did not at first include engaging in sex with the boys as it was only the theoretical part of the course. The female instructor employed touching techniques but she was able to give her pupils full knowledge of sexual relationships. Training in the mystery of love-making was of such importance that no man was allowed to marry until he had completed the course.

When the theory was over, the boys had to undergo circumcision. Some time after that, the boys passed the final stage of initiation. This time each boy had to have real sexual intercourse with his female instructor. The boy was then considered an adult and could marry.

The female instructor, who could even be described as a call-girl, had great respect from the community. She was never paid for her service. She was easily recognised as she wore earrings made of turtle shells and her face was painted to distinguish her from other women in the village. There was not the slightest ill-feeling or stigma attached to her profession and if she decided to marry she was said to become a respectable wife.

6.
Sexual Rites in India

Power of the Living Phallus

Siva, one of the principal Hindu gods, is often represented by the lingam, that is a phallus which is always erect. Siva is said to particularly like being worshipped under this unusual emblem. Lingams vary in size and appearance; they can be as small as a fist or as tall as a tree. The phallic effigy can be an elaborate stone sculpture or it can be a simple effigy made of moulded sand. It is even occasionally made of cow dung.

Among members of some cults the phallus of a living person is an object of worship. According to Benjamin Walker: 'In some cases the member of a guru is kissed and adored by his followers. Similarly, the phallus of a naked sadhu is an object of reverence, and women desirous of bearing children render osculatory homage to the organs of the holy ones to make them fertile'. As B. Z. Goldberg reported in 1931, the priests of Kanara sometimes walked along the streets nude, ringing bells, and women kissed their sexual organ.

There is a fascinating legend about the origin of Hindu phallism. It is said that the great Siva once engaged in sexual intercourse in the presence of Brahma, Vishnu and Yashita. But later he became so ashamed of what he had done that he castrated himself and ordered that the organ of his lust 'should henceforth be worshipped'.

In Siva's temples, the lingam is traditionally set in the yoni, the female sexual organ. Lingams can be seen inside the Hindu temples and in their vicinity and even by roads in the forests.

Every day the devotees of Siva make offerings of flowers, incense and fruits to their own stone or metal emblems of the lingam and yoni. Similar offerings are rendered to lingams found in temples.

Devotion to Siva's symbol is often expressed by pouring water or milk over it. A vessel with liquid is suspended over the lingam so that the liquid drips continuously onto it. In some places this liquid is collected and for therapeutic purposes sold to believers as 'Siva's seed'.

Phallic images are believed to have miraculous power. Women who cannot conceive touch certain lingams to remove their barrenness and they may travel many miles to find a particular lingam. According to W. D. O'Flaherty, 'Young girls often build lingams of sand on the banks of a river, in hope of obtaining a fine husband like Siva'.

The number of lingams in a temple may be significant, too. Sixty-four huge lingams spring from yoni platforms around the temple at Pashupatinath in Nepal. Inside the temple is the most impressive lingam in Nepal. But before a devotee worships the famous lingam, he reverently touches the testicles of a sacred bull whose horns and tail are made of gold. This impressive bull is some 1.5 metres high and about 3 metres long. The famous lingam is about one metre high. It is made of black stone. Five faces of the Lord Siva are carved on its surface.

People are not allowed to touch the sacred lingam but they worship it by pouring milk or water and offering flowers. Only a high priest of the temple has the privilege of touching the famous lingam. He undresses the lingam every day, bathes it and then dresses it again. He even symbolically feeds the great phallic effigy.

Another famous Hindu temple is the eleventh-century temple at Tanjore which is said to have a room known as the Hall of a Thousand Lingams.

Among many impressive lingams in India, the most famous is the one in Amarnath Cave in Pahalgam, Kashmir. It is not man-made, but a natural object in the shape of a human phallus. Believed to have been created miraculously, it is in fact a huge stalagmite formed by water constantly dripping in a cold cave. This remarkable symbol of the great Siva is so popular that people travel from the most distant regions of India to pay homage. As many as 30,000 pilgrims may assemble on the route to the famous 'shrine', especially in seasons when the phallic effigy is at its tallest. People hurry up in order to reach the famous cave in time as they are aware that the lingam can shrink when the weather warms up. Sometimes the famous stalagmite is only some 30 cm high.

Celebrations during which phallic effigies were carried along the streets by devotees were in the past very common in India.

Women of the Ambig caste of Dharwar used to have a very distinctive phallic figure of the deity called Jokamar, represented as a man 'whose private parts were three times as large as the rest of his body'. This impressive effigy of the deity of procreation was carried during a special ceremony from one house to another and people sang in front of each house in honour of the deity and were given small gifts in return.

The members of the Indian caste, Virashaiva, are offered small lingams during their initiation ceremony. They put this effigy in a small silver box and wear it on their neck. Whenever they pray, the tiny lingam is held in the hand.

Worship of the Female Sexual Organ

The male sexual organ is an object of worship in India and Nepal. Siva's spouse Parvati, in the form of the yoni, the female sexual organ is also worshipped. She is worshipped alone or with Siva's lingam (phallus).

Some sects, known as the Left-hand Tantrics worship the yoni of a nude woman. In a special ceremony she sits before worshippers with her legs apart. B. Walker notes 'some tantric sects believe that a man can attain the highest bliss by concentrating on the soul seated in the female sexual organ'. Members of tantric sects, which are outgrowths of Buddhism, liken paradise to the yoni, and they say that Buddha is 'dwelling in the vagina of the female in the name of semen'.

A symbol of the yoni may be a shell, a ring stone or a so-called female stone which have natural perforations through them. If a man finds a stone which fits his own penis he consecrates the stone and wears it thus on his organ secured by a piece of string. These stones are believed to possess the spirit of the goddess and are said to have magical properties.

Some small and hollow stones are considered sacred, but as B. Walker explains; 'Large rock formations with holes in them are regarded as sacred and children, old people, the sterile, the pregnant, the sick, are made to crawl through the hole, and are regarded as born again, purified, or absolved from sin after this procedure'.

There are some temples in India which are exclusively dedicated to the worship of yoni. The most famous is the one in the region of Assam known as Kamarupa. It was erected in the area where Siva is believed to have had secret sex with Sati (later reborn as

Parvati). After her death, while he was carrying her, her genitals fell on the ground in this place. There is no image of the goddess in this temple, but in its depths there is a cleft in the rock. This is worshipped as the yoni of Sati. A natural spring within the cave keeps the cleft moist.

Extensive human sacrifice was practised in honour of the goddess Sati. It was terminated in 1832 when the British made it illegal. The sacrificed people were all volunteers and belonged to a class of men called Bhogi. When this temple was built in 1565, the heads of 140 men were offered to the demanding goddess on salvers made of copper.

Intercourse with a God

In some temples in India in the past gods were said to have the miraculous power to cure barrenness in women. One of the most famous was the temple of Tirupati in the Carnatic. Women from various parts of India made their pilgrimages in the hope that they would be cured by the god Venkateswara (one of the names for Vishnu). On disclosing to the temple manager the object of her visit, the woman was advised that if she spent a night inside the temple, the god, touched by her devotion, might visit her and grant her wish to conceive. In fact it was a temple priest who impersonated the god and who had sex with her. As A. J. A. Dubois tells us: 'The following morning these detestable hypocrites, pretending complete ignorance of what had passed, made due inquiries into all details . . . congratulated them upon the reception they met from the god . . . ' Convinced that they had had the privilege of intercourse with the god, the happy women returned home 'flattering themselves that they will soon procure their husbands the honour of paternity'.

This strange custom prevailed in India until the early twentieth century. The belief that gods can have sex with mortals was also common in ancient Babylon. For example, at the temple dedicated to the god Marduk, there was a special chamber into which a beautiful girl was invited by the temple's priests. Lying on the couch at night, the girl expected the divine lover to come and have sex with her. Her wish was always fulfilled. It was of course one of the temple's priests who played the role of the god for his own pleasure.

Left-hand Lovers

Among certain sects in the East, sexual intercourse is the principal means of achieving spiritual enlightenment and salvation. It is believed to enable sect followers to perceive true reality.

These sects are referred to as Left-hand Tantrics. They are found in Nepal, Bhutan and India. Although the sects are an out-growth of Hinduism, they are opposed to the Vedas, Hindu sacred writings, and therefore despised by Hindus.

As Left-hand Tantrics do not engage in sexual union for gratification, they choose partners irrespective of whether they like each other or not. Sometimes sexual partners are drawn by lot. In fact a man would even prefer an ugly partner to a more attractive one in the belief that he would be better able to concentrate in his efforts to reach the ultimate reality by means of sexual union.

The Left-hand Tantrics practise a peculiar sexual ritual called lotus worship. It is performed under the influence of a hallucinogenic drug. Sitting together on the floor, the participants form a circle. Each female sits on the left of the male partner, hence the term 'Left-hand Tantrism'. The middle of the circle is occupied by the chief male celebrant. Beside him sits a naked lady. With her private parts fully exposed this woman is regarded by all present as a priestess. Her body is ritually washed with wine while the chief celebrant performs ritual chants. It is believed that at this time the Goddess of Nature enters the priestess's body. Miraculously changed into a deity, she is now worshipped and caressed by all members. Finally, the chief male celebrant makes love to this temporary goddess and the rest of the participants form pairs and also engage in sexual unions.

But for some Left-hand Tantrics, sexual intercourse with an unknown woman is considered insufficient 'to gain full enlightenment'. Instead, they engage in ritual union with close family members such as a sister or even a daughter.

Although many tantric sects accept the general philosophy of sexual intercourse in attaining individual enlightenment, some believe that symbolic sexual union can be equally effective. The female partners sit during the meeting on the right-hand side of the males. They call themselves Right-hand Tantrics. Instead of sexual intercourse there is just embracing, caressing and interchange of flowers between the partners.

Left-hand Tantrism is also practised by some sects in Tibet.

These are a deviant form of Buddhism and are despised by Buddhists.

Deviant groups which glorify illicit sex while at the same time accepting some tenets of Christianity, crop up from time to time in Western countries.

7.
Sex and Fertility

Penis as Implement

Incredibly, in some cultures people believed that sexual intercourse was necessary to make the soil fertile. Small wonder that many peculiar customs have evolved in which sexual acts played an essential role. The custom of the Pipele Indians in Central America was that just before the first seeds were sown in the ground real sexual intercourse had to be performed in the field to ensure the fertility of the soil. It was thought that the more vigorous such love-making, the better would be its influence on the plants' growth. A few days before sowing, the chosen couples were placed in isolation so that their sexual desire would be strengthened and on the night before planting they might indulge their passions to the fullest. There was no shame in such an act and the sexual union was encouraged by local priests who considered this to be the married couple's religious duty. It was regarded as very hazardous to sow seed before the important rite had been performed.

Among the Baganda, of East Africa, there was a belief in the relationship between sexual intercourse and fertility of the soil. Thus a sterile woman was sent away because it was believed that she would prevent her husband's garden from yielding. On the other hand, a couple who had twins were considered to have extraordinary fertility which could be transmitted to plants. As the plantain was the main source of food for the community, a special ritual was usually performed to 'force' these plants to bear better fruits. In this rite the twins' mother was taken to a special place where she had to lie on her back in the grass, while a plantain flower was placed on her private parts. Her husband's duty was then to knock the flower down. The man had to perform this duty with his penis. Then the couple were invited to perform ritual dances in the plantain gardens of their friends.

In order for the soil to become fertile in some cultures the copulation of a few selected couples was not enough. Instead, the ritual copulation of all adults in the community was required. Such a custom was practised by the Oraon, an aboriginal tribe of the Chotanagpur plateau in India. In their fertility ceremony the people re-enacted the sacred marriage of the sun god with the earth goddess in spring. The ceremony began with the intercourse of the priest and his wife. This was followed by an incredible sexual orgy of all who participated in the rite.

Sexual orgies were also practised on some of the islands near Timor (Leti and Sermata groups) in order to make the soil fertile and to ensure general prosperity. These rites took place each year, at the beginning of the rainy season.

Sometimes, however, it was not sexual intercourse but sexual organs which were part of a magical formula to ensure the fertility of the soil. In the case of Lango (a Ugandan tribe) it was a truly bizarre formula.

Sexual organs were obtained by raiding and killing a man and a dog from a neighbouring tribe. The scrotum of the man and that of the dog were then stuffed with millet seed. A rain dance followed, and then each man took home with him some of the millet seeds. Before sowing, the farmers mixed this magical millet with ordinary millet. The tribesmen were convinced that their magic worked well.

Sexual Race

At first sight it appears that there cannot be any connection between nakedness and agriculture. However, in a number of cultures it was believed that the presence of a naked woman at the crucial moment of sowing would have a positive effect on crop yield. In fact, even at the turn of this century, in what used to be Eastern Prussia, the custom was for women to go into the field naked, and in this manner to sow peas to ensure good yield.

A strong element of eroticism could also be detected in the agricultural customs of Finland. There, women used to cover seeds in a cloth which had been worn during menstruation. It could also be a shoe of a prostitute or a stocking of an illegitimate child. People believed that this custom augmented the fertility of the crop.

The Finns used to believe that the gender who sowed the seeds had an important impact on the crop's yield. While beetroot sown by women was said to be sweet, that sown by men was said to be bitter. Fertility of women engaged in sowing was so important that in the past a Finnish woman feeding a baby would sprinkle the furrows with a few drops of her own milk before planting the seeds in the field.

In Germany, too, women were responsible for sowing seeds and the women preferred were those who were pregnant.

In Finland and Estonia women used to sow seeds naked. While they did this, they used to pray: 'Lord, I am naked! Bless my flax!'

In Estonia nakedness was also involved in preparing the soil. To ensure a good harvest it was necessary for farmers to be naked while ploughing and harrowing. In Ukraine, on a special day just before sowing grain, it was customary for young married couples to arrive at the field and roll over on the ground several times in the belief that such an act would promote the growth of crops.

The relationship between naked women and soil fertility was also believed in by the Hindus. They used to believe that when the fertility of the soil was threatened by drought, it could only be restored if women would go out naked and pull a plough through the fields before sowing.

The Indians of Peru, Chile, and Nicaragua also had peculiar customs linking nakedness with soil fertility. Special festivals were organised for this purpose. Before the celebrations, long periods of fasting and sexual abstinence were observed. These festivals were organised at the time of sowing seeds, and when avocados ripened. All the participants were completely naked; they took part in a race in which every man was supposed to catch a woman and have sex with her. This custom was witnessed by the Europeans in the seventeenth century.

Sexy Yams

In many societies the presence of a naked woman in the field was believed to have a miraculous effect on the harvest, but the opposite view was held by others. Among the Abelam of Sepik River (Papua New Guinea) for instance, it was considered disastrous for a woman to have any contact with yams (their main crop). Women were strictly excluded from yam gardens. And men growing the yams had to observe a complete taboo on sex since it would hurt the plants. It is hard to believe, but men refrained from having sex for about six months, half of each year, from planting to harvesting.

A good yam specimen was displayed during harvest festival and it was a proof of its owner's masculinity. All the men took part in a competition which the owner of the largest yam won. Men who consecutively produced the largest specimens acquired the highest prestige and were called Big Men.

Yams collected for competition were decorated and painted in a special way. Specimens which were forked, and had two 'legs', were considered to be of female gender. To emphasise this, the appropriate sexual organ was painted in the proper place. Normal yams were said to be male and had a picture of a lizard painted on them. Some of the tubers displayed were real giants as they could be nearly 3.5 m long. Special registers of yams were kept to exclude forgery.

During the festival men used to offer each other their best yams and the man who gave the bigger yam was said to be superior to his partner. Although the offering did not make the loser happy, it was nevertheless considered to be an act of good will.

An offer of a big yam outside festival time was, however, a truly unfriendly act. It signified that the giver accused the man of having sex with the giver's wife. The offer meant that his wife's lover was too lazy to be able to grow a yam specimen of a decent size.

8.
Sex and Human Sacrifice

Extraordinary Sacrifice

The extraordinary fertility deity on Mer Island (Torres Strait) was called Waiet. The effigy of this deity was presented in the form of a man-like figure with outstretched arms. It had no legs as it was believed that this god had already found his place so he would not need to move. The face of the god was made of a piece of a turtle shell which had eyes, mouth and nostrils carved to resemble a man. The headdress was made of fern feathers dipped in blood. To emphasise the evil nature of this god a string of red-painted human rib bones was hung from his forehead. Human arm and leg bones were attached to his waist. Small wonder that the deity with such a gruesome appearance demanded a very special sacrifice.

The sacrifice was truly incredible. During an eight day celebration in honour of the deity, men's sexual organs were sacrificed each day. Before the ritual killing the victim's body was marked by the priests so that the desired portion of flesh could be consumed after killing. Before the man was slain the priest cut off the victim's sexual organs which were then placed on the extended palms of the idol.

When the sacrificial rites were over, the collected sexual organs were placed on the top of the deity's head. Then it was time for a feast. The priests and their assistants cut the selected body parts from the victim's body, cooked and ate them. During this macabre feast, the chief priest would assure the gathered people that the god had accepted the sacrifice and now demanded that each woman become his bride. Then the chief priest would select a woman for his pleasure and the others would follow in order of seniority.

The sexual orgy in honour of the deity continued all night. Everybody present participated.

Although such behaviour seems strange, there was a reason for it. There were frequent battles with hostile neighbouring tribes in which many young men perished and it was necessary to maintain a high birth rate to survive. As many local men were sterile, the custom of organising a sexual orgy after celebrations was valuable. It was a useful opportunity for fertile men to copulate with several women and make them pregnant.

Sacrifice of Phallic Blood

The ancient Mayas believed that their gods cherished most the blood obtained from male sexual organs. It was customary, therefore, that before a male victim was ritually killed his genitals were wounded first in order to collect the precious blood. The blood dropping from the wounded penis was then smeared on the god's effigy nearby. This strange ritual was followed by a 'normal sacrifice'. The victim, who was painted blue, was sacrificed in a special rite known as the arrow ceremony; the priest's assistants one by one shot their arrows at the naked chest of the victim.

Fresh blood obtained from a man's penis was so precious as a means of propitiating the gods that every man used to offer blood from his own penis.

This unusual custom was observed by the Franciscan, Diego de Landa, who in the sixteenth century studied the Maya religion and customs. He reported in 1566 that ordinary men used to split the superfluous part of their penis, cutting it and fraying it to obtain sufficient blood as a sacrifice to gods. He said, 'Some Mayas had holes drilled completely through their penis . . . obliquely, from side to side and through this hole they passed a cord. With a long thin cord inside their penis they performed their extraordinary dance during which the flowing blood was caught and then the idol was anointed with it'.

Occasionally this sacrifice of blood was performed as an open ritual. As one eyewitness of the rite said: 'I saw the sacrifice. They took a chisel and wooden mallet, laced the one who had sacrificed himself on a smooth stone slab, took out the penis and made three cuts into it an inch long in the centre . . . all the time they murmured incantations'.

Fresh blood from male genitals was believed to have the power to propitiate their gods, but blood from other parts of the body was also offered. People deliberately pierced their ears, lips or cheeks and the blood obtained in this way was smeared on the god's image. Even tongues were occasionally pierced to collect blood for the gods.

———

9.

Sexual Customs in Europe

Phallic Worship

Phallic worship was not confined to Africa and Asia; it was also found in so-called 'enlightened' Europe. The ancient Greek goddess of love, Aphrodite, was represented by images of sexual organs. Those who were initiated into her cult were given an image of a human phallus and her temple in Corinth was the sacred place for local prostitutes.

Priapus, said to be the son of Dionysius and Aphrodite, was regarded as the guardian of fields, gardens and vineyards and protector of domestic animals. Wooden figures of naked Priapus with an enormous erect penis were a common sight in gardens and fields. Since Priapus was also the protector of graves his 'indecent' images were seen on tombstones, too.

In ancient Rome the worship of the goddess of virginity, Diana, involved the people watching sexual intercourse performed by a priest with a prostitute on the stage of the temple.

The Romans also worshipped as a god the isolated phallus, whom they called Mutunus or Tutunus. This god was believed to be responsible for the fertility of both men and women. According to custom, before the wedding night, young brides had to visit the idol of this phallic deity. The girl had her head covered with a veil and she had to sit on the huge phallus of the deity's statue. The idol was also visited by married but childless couples hoping to conceive.

Phallic images were not only associated with sex and human reproduction. Ancient Greeks and Romans were afraid of the evil eye. The way to prevent harm was to depict everywhere images of genitals. It was believed that the evil eye was so fascinated by them that it would look only at this image and hence would be harmless to the person who wore an amulet depicting sexual organs.

Images of genitals could be seen on the walls of houses, on gate posts and on clothing. Sometimes the image was a phallus with claws and wings. Most amulets depicted the phallus, but some illustrated the vulva in the form of a fig. Even small children used to have phallic amulets hanging around their necks.

In ancient Greece and Rome the human phallus was believed to possess the magical power to help in battle. Greek and Etruscan warriors wore helmets, greaves and breast-plates but deliberately left their genitals uncovered. When they had killed an enemy warrior, they cut off his penis and used it as a trophy.

Organ of Sin

Among some religious sects which claimed to be Christian there were cruel groups which demanded that members castrate themselves as a sacrifice to God. They claimed that the male sexual organ was created for sin, and that elimination of it was the best way to achieve purity of soul. It was hazardous even to meet members of such sects because in the name of God they were ready to castrate non-believers.

One such sect, born in Europe in the middle of the third century AD, was especially active. They were proud of having cut off some 700 organs of sin in just one year. The gruesome sect was established by a man named Valerian and the sect members called themselves Valerians. The sect ceased to exist after its founder died.

The idea of religious castration survived though and was resurrected in the early eighteenth century, this time in Russia. Lupkin, the sect leader was enthusiastically prosecuted for his deeds. He was captured by the police and executed. Later, to completely eradicate his sect Czarina Anna Ivanovna ordered his body to be dug up and reburied in an unmarked grave.

Another sect of castrators established in Russia in 1771 by Konradij Selivanov were named Skoptsi. The leader of the sect called himself Czar Peter III and his followers thought him to be more important than his 'brother' Jesus Christ. The Skoptsi movement was widespread in Russia as late as the second half of the nineteenth century. Skoptsi were also active in Rumania where in three major cities they had some 20,000 members.

The sect leader maintained that both he and Christ were eunuchs as they had sacrificed their genitals. He claimed that the statement about necessity of castration had been suppressed from the Holy Scripture. In his view the New Testament's phrase about the 'baptism by fire' meant 'castration'.

During the early years of the sect castration was performed in the most cruel way possible: by burning the testicles with a white hot iron. Later, the method was replaced by cutting out the testicles. The sect divided its initiates into two categories: those who had their testicles removed, and the more 'advanced' initiates whose penis was amputated as well. This painful operation was performed using a razor or knife, scissors, glass or even an axe.

In some big cities in Russia, e.g. Moscow, there was even a special piece of furniture shaped like a cross used for castration. Some members of the sect castrated their own children to please the god and 'to destroy the sinful organ of their sons'.

These incredible practices were not restricted to men. Members of the sect also believed that removal of female genitals was necessary for the same reasons.

Female sexual organs, that is clitoris and labia minor, were amputated. Some female devotees also sacrificed their nipples which were removed by cutting or burning. Some 'pious' women removed the whole breast.

The members of the Skoptsi sect were so mad that in a special ceremony held before Easter they 'consumed' female breasts severed from fifteen or sixteen year old girls. As one author noted: 'The breast was cut into small pieces on a silver dish and all members who were present and who by this time had divested themselves of all garments except a shirt, had to eat it'.

Devil's Phallus

European witches of the past claimed to have had sexual intercourse with the Devil. They were even able to describe his sexual organ in detail. According to a witch called Isobel Gowdie who was sentenced in 1662: 'His members are exceeding great and long; no man's members are so long and as big as they are . . . [he is] a meikle, black rough man, very cold; and I found his nature as cold within me as spring-well water . . . He is abler for us that way than any man can be, only he is heavy like a malt-sack'. Other witches also claimed that the Devil's penis was very long and either very thick or thin; it was always erect and made of horn or iron.

How was it possible for a witch to describe the Devil's sexual organ in such detail? The answer is that the witches' meetings were always presided over by a man in disguise who had sex with all the women there, and there could be up to twelve witches present. The only possibility was that the stand-in Devil must have had an artificial penis. And as the witches who attended the secret meeting with the Devil were under the influence of hallucinogenic potions, they could easily be convinced that they had had intercourse with the Devil.

These witches were known for their gruesome rituals. For example, their sacrifices involved killing animals such as goats or hens and even human babies. A baby for sacrifice could be the witch's stillborn child or may have been stolen from a mother. Even newly buried babies were occasionally used. According to a report in 1661 a baby was stolen from a grave and eaten ritually by witches. She said 'they took pieces thereof, as the feet, hands, a pairt of the head, and a pairt of the buttock, and they made a py thereof, that they might eat it, that by this means they might never make a confession (as they thought) of their witchcrafts'.

It was believed that witches had the power to fly, could inflict madness and illness of every kind and even death upon their victims. The main weapon of the witch was her evil eye; just her glance from a distance with evil intent was said to be lethal.

Thousands of witches accused of using the evil eye to cast horrific spells were executed during the witch hunts in sixteenth and seventeenth century Europe. It was assumed that the witches' magic power was the result of a compact with the Devil.

Even the judges who prosecuted them and sentenced them to death by torture were afraid of their evil eye. In the *Malleus Male-ficarum*, a special handbook for the Inquisition in Europe, a special warning was provided that 'there are witches who can bewitch their judges by a mere look or glance from their eyes . . '. Small wonder that it was customary for witches to be led backwards into court to prevent them using their malevolent glances on the judge.

Phallic Saints

Some early Christians did not entirely give up their pagan beliefs. They mixed their new faith with paganism by ascribing to some Christian saints the powers previously attributed to pagan gods.

This was especially the case in medieval France where a number of phallic saints' peculiar images could be seen in some local churches. Carved images of such saints often had a long stag horn passed through a hole in the lower part of the body symbolising the penis. At Orange in France, the statue of St Eutropius had a large wooden phallus which was covered with leather.

A large number of wooden effigies of the phallus of St Foutin could be seen in the Middle Ages in France and these phalli were scraped by sterile women who made a concoction from the shavings in the belief that drinking it would help them to conceive. Similarly, to restore virility to weak husbands, the same concoction was given them to drink.

Offerings given to the phallic saints at Varailles in Provence in France were incredible. They were waxen images of the sexual parts of men and women. Another interesting custom prevailed at Embrun in the Alps in the Middle Ages. Worship of the sacred phallus was performed by pouring wine on top of the phallic effigy and collecting it after washing. This wine was considered sacred. It was kept for a long time in a large vessel until it soured. It was then drunk by women in the belief that it would enhance their fertility.

Phallic images could be seen in French churches as late as the French Revolution of 1789. They were especially common on the portico of the cathedral of Toulouse and in a number of churches in the region of Bordeaux.

In some parts of France until the eighteenth century phallic images were linked with Christian festivals. At Saintonge, locals made small cakes in the form of a phallus which were used as offerings at Easter. In Saintes, Palm Sunday was known to the locals as the festival of the penis. In the procession women and children used to carry phalli made of bread at the end of their palm branches. Each phallus was then blessed by the priest and preserved until the next year as an amulet. Similar customs were recorded from elsewhere in France. They were obviously modified left-overs from ancient times.

During the early Christian era some young women used to sit on a stone phallus in order to get fertile as had been done in ancient Rome. Amulets with sexual motifs which were common in ancient Greece and Rome continued to be popular in the Middle Ages in Europe. Some of these amulets were made in the form of a phallus with wings and claws, while others showed a female riding a phallus which had man's legs. They were used as protection against evil.

10.
Prostitution

Compulsory Prostitution

The Babylonian goddess of love, Mylitta, demanded a peculiar
sacrifice. According to Herodotus, the ancient historian, every
woman born in Babylon had once in her life to make a sacrifice
to the goddess of love. This extraordinary sacrifice was described
by Herodotus as a most shameful custom. It required every woman
at least once to sit in the precinct of the temple devoted to Mylitta
and have sex with a stranger. He wrote: 'A woman who has once
taken her seat is not allowed to return home until one of the
strangers throws a silver coin into her lap, and takes her with him
beyond the holy ground. When he throws the coin he says these
words: "The goddess Mylitta prosper thee".'

Even if the coin was the smallest size the woman was forbidden
by law to refuse it. Once it was thrown into her lap it was regarded
as sacred. The woman had to go with the first stranger who threw
her a coin. After having sex with the stranger, she returned home
and as a rule she would never prostitute herself again.

While for an attractive woman there was no problem in fulfilling
her religious duty, the less attractive or ugly had to stay a long
time before they were able to fulfil their obligation. Some had
to wait for up to four years.

The temple dedicated to the goddess of love was always full
of people. As Herodotus tells us: 'Lines of cords mark out paths
in all directions among the women, and strangers pass along them
to make their choice'. While some poorer women arrived on foot,
wealthier ones arrived in covered carriages, and were 'followed
by a goodly train of attendants, and there take their station'. But

there is no evidence that all the Babylonian women who arrived at the temple were virgins. Herodotus does not mention this in his description of the practice.

In a similar rite performed in Baalbek (now Lebanon) in ancient times, virgin girls had to show their devotion to the goddess of love by means of temporary prostitution to a stranger. It was a single act of prostitution arranged at the precinct of the temple devoted to the goddess Astarte. But after that, chastity was required before marriage. This form of religious prostitution was also known in ancient Egypt, but there it was only a duty of the daughters of the nobility.

Temporary prostitution was also a custom in ancient Cyprus. Parents sent their daughters to the seashore before marriage where they were obliged to prostitute themselves. The aim of this custom was to collect sufficient money for their marriage but also to make offerings to the goddess of love 'for the preservation of their chastity in time to come'.

Japanese God of Prostitution

Inari is the Japanese god of prostitution. J. F. Embree noted in 1946: 'Inari is a god of crops, more especially of rice, and, as such many farmers have him in their houses. He is also the god of prostitutes and geisha, and as such he is enshrined in every geisha house and brothel'. Inari shrines are visited regularly by the prostitutes to pay their respects.

Strange customs were associated with prostitutes. Once a year in a Tokyo suburb there was a street procession of beautiful prostitutes. As H. Ploss and M. Bartels noted in 1935: 'By red and white rope they drew the carriage on which stood a gigantic flower basket; in it was a gorgeously coloured bouquet of peonies, camellias, tiger-lilies, chrysanthemums and sprays of cherry blossom. This vehicle was followed by the beauties. In front of each were two richly dressed children, the girls wearing garlands, golden tassels, butterflies or some finery in their hair; while the boys had all kinds of strange tonsures. Behind these little satellites, came one at a time, truly beautiful maidens . . . in wonderfully embroidered garments of silk brocade of a richness in material and a taste in colour such as I have never seen . . . Holding the train of their rich garments across their breasts with their delicate hands [they] went ceremoniously and gravely along the streets without a trace of frivolity'.

Japan was the only country in the world where such parades took place.

Another strange celebration took place in November each year. As D. Sladen and N. Lorimer wrote in 1905: 'It is celebrated on the cock days in November, sometimes twice and sometimes thrice, according to the number of cock days happening to be in the same month . . . As a rule, on those fete days all the prostitute quarters open every gate and receive visitors, who seize the occasion to see their love objects—beautifully dressed harlots'.

A fete in honour of the god Inari took place annually in September. This celebration took the form of a play and dance called Niwaka. 'On the occasion, the professional buffoons belonging to the infamous quarter, as well as the singing and dancing girls, all in disguise, perform low comedy, usually men in women's and women in men's dress. Some ten or twenty singing girls, wearing men's clothes, draw a gigantic lion-head made of wood, unitedly singing barbarous songs, accompanied with strange music . . .'.

There was also an annual festival in honour of a famous prostitute called Tamagiku who had died. 'During the festival known as the Feast of Lanterns the whole quarter wherein she dwelt while living lamented over the loss of her, and every house hanged out a lantern, upon which a kind of elegy was written for her, in order to console the dead spirit of her. This being the origin of the celebration, it has now lost the mournful character entirely, and taken a licentious character'.

11.
Sex and Marriage

Marriage to a Fruit

One would normally expect a marriage to involve the union of two human beings. In certain societies, however, there is a peculiar marriage in which a girl does not marry a person but an object. Among the Newar people of Nepal, there is a custom that a young girl first marries a fruit.

In this unusual marriage a green fruit of the wood-apple tree (*Aegle marmelos*), called Bel fruit, is the bridegroom. The marriage is called 'Ihin' and is of course a symbolic union, but it has strong binding power since the fruit symbolises the god Vishnu. Marriage to such an immortal deity is celebrated with as much splendour as a normal wedding.

Girls who are going to marry the god are usually between five and twelve and they have not reached puberty. Since such a wedding takes place only once a year many girls can participate in the same wedding ceremony. The astrological data are considered and the date of the wedding is fixed in advance. The girls are bathed and beautifully dressed in a special sari so that the small brides look most attractive. As a sign of good luck a porcupine's spine is often inserted in the hair of the bride.

The Bel fruit for the marriage is carefully chosen so as it is not misshapen or damaged. It is believed that if the fruit chosen is unsuitable, the girl's future mortal husband will be dishonest and ugly. So the best fruits with a typical pear-like shape are selected and then adorned to make attractive 'grooms'.

A special altar is constructed for the wedding ceremony. Banana trees are usually placed at the four corners and the canopy for

the altar is made of a red cloth. The brides sit accompanied by
their parents. The fruit-bridegroom cannot be seen at this initial
stage of the ceremony since it is bedecked. After the priest has
performed the purification rituals and specified chanting, he places
each Bel fruit on a separate plate and the bride's father offers his
daughter to the fruit which is her symbolic bridegroom.

After the ceremony the Bel fruit is carefully preserved by the
elders of the family of the bride. It is usually placed on the roof
of the house. It is believed that if such a Bel fruit is broken after
marriage the future mortal husband of the girl would die at a young
age. After the wedding a great community feast commences in
which hundreds of invited guests can participate.

When the girl who was married to a Bel fruit reaches puberty
she is ready for her second marriage which is performed once
a proper candidate is found.

Despite the marriage to a fruit being only a symbolic union,
it has a powerful binding force as it is a marriage to a god who
is immortal. The strange marriage has a special advantage to a
married woman though. In the event of the early death of her
real husband, a woman married to a fruit is not obliged to submit
to the harsh Hindu laws of widowhood. The widowed woman can
still consider herself not to be a real widow because of her still
valid first marriage. Such a woman can therefore remarry without
problems.

Marriage to a Tree

Although it appears bizarre for a man to marry a tree, such marriages
do occur. In fact problems can be solved through such a peculiar
marriage. For example, the Hindus of Punjab have the custom that
a man who was already married twice cannot take another wife,
because he is forbidden to marry three times. But he is allowed
to marry for the fourth time. Such a hindrance can be easily removed
by ritual marriage to a tree. In such a case the bridegroom marries
a tree (usually a babul tree, *Acacia arabica*) which is considered
to be his third wife. Having done this a man can now marry another
woman in the normal way as his next wife. She is regarded as
his fourth spouse which is permitted by custom.

In other parts of India such as Madras, a tree marriage is commonly
practised to overcome the traditional law forbidding a younger
brother from marrying before his elder brother. It sometimes

happens that an older brother remains single for a long time or decides not to marry at all. A younger brother might have to wait for a long time for his turn to marry or may have no chance to marry at all. To remove the obstacle, it is arranged for the elder brother to marry a tree. A plantain tree is usually chosen as the bride. But when the tree wedding is over another strange rite follows. The local priest chops down the 'wedded' tree which is then pronounced dead. It is then mourned by the temporary husband and family as if it were his real wife. In this odd way the elder brother has lost his wife and become a widower, but the young brother is now free to get married.

Marriage to a plant is also customary for women who cannot find a husband. The daughter of a courtesan normally cannot marry but may have a ritual husband by marrying a living plant. She can choose as her groom a flowering plant growing in her house. As wife to this plant it is customary for her to care for her 'husband' in a special way. When the plant dies she mourns as if it were a real person.

It may sound unusual but there is also the custom in India to marry not only a person to a tree, but to marry two trees to each other. This marriage takes place for entirely different reasons. It is arranged by a childless couple in an effort to conceive. Two different trees are planted together by the childless couple. The wife usually plants a small fig tree, while the husband chooses a young mango tree. The stems are joined together to make them a 'married couple'. The childless couple who perform the ritual walk around the 'married' trees in the belief that these magically combined trees will make the woman fertile. Such 'married' trees are fenced and cared for by the couple and watered for many years. If one of the 'married' trees dies this is considered a bad omen for the woman.

Not only plants are chosen as marriage partners. There are cases when a girl marries a living or even non-living object. The Gonds who live in Bastar (central India), believe that if a husband is killed by a tiger his widow must not marry again because the husband's spirit has entered the tiger's body and will try to kill the man whom she marries. To prevent this, the widow must first ritually marry a dog or a weapon.

By marrying a dog or a weapon the first husband's spirit will either kill the dog or will himself be killed by the weapon.

Marriage to an object also existed elsewhere; among the Maritime Koryaks of Siberia the custom was that an adult man could marry a stone. There was no wedding ceremony at all. The man simply chose the most 'handsome' looking stone, put clothes on it and placed his peculiar 'bride' in his bed. Unlike the Bel fruit, there was even some sexual connotation in a stone marriage since the man treated the stone as a human, caressing it as if it were a real woman.

Marriages to objects were known too in Mongolia. A stranger for whose sexual pleasure a girl was offered by her father, had to leave his belt as a gift. It was the special gift of a man who might never return. If the girl got pregnant as a result of this sexual hospitality there was no problem because she then simply married the belt which symbolised her husband. On the other hand, if a girl had sex with a stranger outside the sexual hospitality arrangement and became pregnant, she was married to a prayer rug.

Marriage to a Ghost

Even more improbable than human marriage to an object seems to be a marriage of the already dead. Such incredible marriages are still practised by some Chinese and are referred to as marriages of ghosts. These strange marriages are also called 'hell marriages'.

Usually in a dream, the ghost of a deceased person informs his still living relatives about his wish to marry. In one case a young woman had a baby boy who died in his infancy. Some twenty years later the same woman had a dream in which a young man claiming to be her deceased son asked: 'Mother, I want to marry a girl, who lives here in the world of shades with me'. Her son then gave her the name and address of the girl's parents. In a dream the mother promised her son to fulfil his wish.

The next day the woman went to the given address where she found the parents of the deceased girl, who, believe it or not, told her that they had had a similar message from their long-dead daughter. The marriage of ghosts later took place, only differing from a normal wedding because the couple was absent. The above event is fully congruent with the Chinese belief according to which deceased children send messages to their living parents from the world of spirits. Since the ghosts' world is similar to our world, they say marriages of ghosts are equally important.

Marriage to a ghost may come as a result of social obligations. In such a case it does not involve mysterious dreams or unusual messages. No contact at all is made with the ghosts. The parents of a dead child wait until their deceased son or daughter is 'old' enough for marriage and then ask a Taoist priest to perform a marriage ceremony. When a suitable partner in the afterworld is found by the priest, the marriage is performed and joins the pair of ghosts for ever.

The ghost may wish, though, to marry a living person. A fascinating case about such a marriage was reported in the Chinese press in 1978. One day while walking in the street in Taipei (Taiwan) a man called Mr Lee saw a little package lying on the street. He picked it up and when he unwrapped it he found a gold engagement ring inside. Immediately a young man approached him and made a rather unexpected request. He said: 'Would you care to marry my older sister, sir?' He explained that his sister who had died many years before had contacted his family in a dream and demanded that they arrange her wedding in the following strange manner. Her brother was to buy a gold ring which was to be put in a small package on the street. The first gentleman who picked it up would become her predestined husband.

Although at first Mr Lee was reluctant, he realised that it might be dangerous to refuse a request from a ghost. So he agreed to the proposed marriage. The marriage ceremony was soon organised by the deceased girl's family. In every detail it was a normal marriage, except that the bride was absent.

In this peculiar wedding the spirit bride was represented by a dummy made of paper and cloth. Her head was a glossy attractive girl's photograph taken from a wall calendar. The head was stuffed with paper and stuck to a strip of wood which formed the backbone of the figure. The arms were made from padded newspaper. The smiling dummy was about one metre tall and was seated during the wedding ceremony.

When the ceremony was over, the newly wed husband had to spend his nuptial night in the bedroom which had belonged to the deceased girl. He stayed the whole night and slept in the bed, but instead of a woman there was a plaque with the engraved name of the ghost girl he married. In this unusual way the marriage of a man to a ghost was 'consummated'. Since Mr Lee was then regarded as a family member, he became a real son-in-law to the girl's parents. He was invited to all family celebrations taking place at home. He continued to pay respects to his ghost wife, and everybody was satisfied with the arrangement.

Marriage of ghosts is even practised among some Christians; Mormons in the USA have the custom of saving a soul by a strange marriage rite. They believe that an unmarried man who has died can be saved, even if during his life he was a non-believer, if he is ritually married to a living Mormon woman.

Goblin's Child

One of the strangest marriage customs in the world was probably that of the Banaro people of New Guinea. The bridegroom did not take part in the wedding ceremony. He was kept imprisoned and watched by his mother's brother so that he could not escape during the ceremony. The wedding ritual involved the defloration of the bride, but this was not done by the groom but by the groom's father.

However, according to tradition, the latter was so ashamed of doing this that he asked his clan friend to do it for him. When they agreed who would perform the defloration, the groom's father conducted the bride of his son to a special hall where his 'helpful' friend was already waiting. The hall was known as the goblin's hall.

There were special bamboo pipes hidden in this hall but the bride was forbidden to look at them, because it was believed that if she did she would die. It was in front of these bamboo pipes that the girl lost her virginity by having sex with the friend of the groom's father. It was then the groom's father's turn to have sex with the bride. When all this had taken place, the marriage ceremony was regarded as completed.

Despite the fact that the man was already considered officially married to the girl, he had to wait until the first child was born before he was allowed to have sexual relations with her. When the child was born the mother asked: 'Where is the father? Who had to do with me?' The husband then answered: 'I am not his father, he is a goblin-child'. Her reply was as follows: 'I did not see that I had intercourse with a goblin'. In this way the strange conversation ended. The couple then moved to a house constructed in the mean time by the patient husband. From then on they could engage freely in sexual intercourse.

The sexual rights of the husband's father over his son's wife continued after the first child was born, but there were certain conditions. First, he could have sex with her only in the goblin's hall, and second, it could only take place on certain occasions. This strange marriage custom was practised as late as 1916.

Marriage to Gods

Marriage of gods to mortals was common in some parts of India. These were official marriages between girls and such important Hindu gods as Siva and Krishna. The marriage was arranged for a girl when she was seven or eight years old. According to one traveller, who described such a marriage ceremony in South Travancore in 1909: 'The priest performs all the marriage ceremonies, following the custom of the Tirukkalyanam Festival, when Siva is represented as marrying Parvati'. During the marriage between girl and deity the girl sat in her wedding dress in the temple facing the deity who was her groom. When the ritual was over the girl was said to have become the wife of a god. She was then taken to her parents' house where marriage festivities resembling those of normal weddings continued for about three days.

The god's spouse was then taken to the temple where she was to serve the god for the rest of her life. The girl was usually deflowered by a temple priest or by an eminent community member. The girl was then trained in erotic dances and became a temple prostitute to serve priests and worshippers. Children born from such sexual relations remained in the temple with their mothers. They helped them in cleaning the temple and also participated in various religious ceremonies.

Girls who married gods and became temple prostitutes did not choose this profession themselves. They were offered by their parents to whom such a marriage was a great honour. The parents often hoped too that in return for their generosity to the god they would be provided with a long awaited son.

In some temples there were so many prostitutes seducing the worshippers that they resembled a brothel more than a place of worship. Pilgrims even complained that the girls hindered them in their worship of the gods.

The women's activity in the temples was considered a normal business. Local authorities even used to tax the girls. In 1927, it was estimated that there were no less than 200,000 temple prostitutes in the state of Madras which had 4 million inhabitants. By the early 1930s, temple prostitution was prohibited by law in many states of India. At present there is officially no temple prostitution. Some authors speculate, though, that temple prostitution still exists in remote parts of India.

Marriage to gods was also known in Haiti. Such marriages were only performed in exceptional cases, when an attractive woman became so intensely sexually active that she was believed to be temporarily possessed by a voodoo god showing his desire to marry her. The marriage ceremony was then performed at the temple by a voodoo priest. The deity was invoked to possess the woman and become her husband. This was an official marriage ceremony during which the bride exchanged rings with the voodoo god personified by a man. It was said that once the strange marriage ceremony was over, the licentious behaviour of the woman would immediately cease.

Violent Night

In every society a newly wedded couple would expect to engage in sexual intercourse during the nuptial night. But this is not always the case. In some countries there is a tradition that a period of abstinence must be strictly observed after the wedding. Such a period may be as short as one night, as among the people of Luzon in the Philippines, or as long as a few months as among the Thligits of North America.

To ensure that such abstinence really is observed by the couple, various methods are employed; the commonest and the simplest is to ask a child or an old woman to sleep between the lovers.

Mere initial abstention from sex is insufficient for the tribe of Bahutu in Rwand (central Africa). Their marriage rites require that the newly wed couple must show hate towards each other. After the wedding ceremony, during the night, the wife who is veiled, goes to the house of her husband which is located near his parental dwelling. Here, the couple start a ferocious fight. The young wife is especially aggressive. She mercilessly slashes and scratches the man she has chosen as her loving husband, treating him as her worst enemy. Fighting continues non-stop throughout the night. It may be so vigorous that the partition walls of the hut are knocked down and its pillars collapse. All this ritual struggle is performed without saying a word.

Although the parents who live close to the hut hear the fighting, they say nothing because the weird behaviour of the newly wed pair is in accordance with Bahutu tradition. The fight ceases at dawn and the wife returns to her parents' house to rest. But the following night the story is repeated.

The fighting may continue for several nights; in some regions it lasts four weeks. When the aggression period is over, the newly wed wife moves for good to her husband's house, and does not return to her parents' house during the day. No fighting takes place; peace and mutual love develop as if nothing had happened. The husband now unveils his 'hidden' wife and the marriage can be consummated in a normal peaceful way. When Bahutu were asked the reason for such strange behaviour just after the wedding, they said that such is the custom. Some anthropologists argue that newly wed aggressiveness symbolises the woman's will to preserve her virginity longer.

Marriage by Capture

In the Aki region of Tosa in Japan, men often used to capture and abduct girls whom they wanted to marry. Before her abduction, however, the man had to apply for permission through the so-called Young Men's Sex Organisation. When he had obtained the consent, together with a few of his close friends, he would abduct the girl by force while she was leaving her house. The captured girl was then kept in a secret place. One of his friends would inform the parents about what had happened, and about the wish of the man to marry their daughter. A special betrothal gift to her parents was offered and they usually agreed to the demand. Some parents, especially the less wealthy, were actually glad that the abduction had taken place as they did not have to pay for the wedding. This strange marriage custom, although officially prohibited because of the violence necessary, continued in some areas of Japan until about 1868.

Sometimes the girl was well acquainted with the young man who wanted to marry her and there was no need for abduction. She usually indicated her desire to marry him by blackening her teeth which was a bridal symbol. But sometimes fraud was employed if a girl was unwilling to marry the man. The young man would blow some teeth-blackening paste into the girl's mouth to make it look to others that she accepted him as a bridegroom.

Taking wives by force was once also common in Europe. There it was marriage by capture without the girl's consent or that of her parents. Such a marriage, involving a violent seizure was legal in England until the reign of Henry VII. It was then prohibited by law, but capture of heiresses was reported in Ireland as late as the eighteenth century.

The practice was so popular in Italy in medieval times that armed guards were employed by wealthy families to protect their young daughters from being abducted.

Marriage by capture was common among the Albanians in some regions till the beginning of the nineteenth century. In some remote regions the custom persisted till the early twentieth century.

The use of violence and coercion as a form of marriage persuasion has been reported among many tribes and people. In some Aboriginal tribes of Australia men used violence and even rape to make a woman their wife. A man usually tried to steal a woman belonging to another tribe. To do so he would prowl around the outskirts of her camp, and wait until the woman left her dwelling. He then attacked her brutally, stunning her with a blow of his club, and dragged her unconscious into the neighbouring bush. Here he waited for his lady to recover from the blow, and then he forced her to follow him home to his community. Here it was customary for a man to rape the captured woman in the presence of his clan. This event confirmed the marriage.

Marriage by capture is still practised among the Araunians of southern Chile. A man who wants to marry a girl of his choice sends his friends on a special mission to the girl's house. While the friends are bargaining with her father, the bridegroom enters the house, catches the girl and takes her away on his horse. As soon as he reaches a special spot in the forest where no one can find them, the girl is regarded as his wife. The marriage is valid even if the abduction was carried out against her parents' will.

In the Purang district of Tibet a girl is captured from her home and carried away by force by a man who wants to marry her. Although confined against her will to a separate house she is treated extremely well. She is given nice clothes, good food and is served by the man who tries to win her love. If the girl refuses to marry her captor, the matter is settled by the village elders. If they permit the marriage, a special day is chosen for the marriage ceremony which involves feasting and heavy drinking.

Embryo Marriage

Many people take it for granted that marriage can only take place when both partners are sufficiently mature to be able to establish a sexual relationship. This is not always the case. Child marriage was regarded as lawful among some Hindu groups.

According to these groups, a girl's father had to marry off his young daughter before she reached puberty. If his daughter remained unmarried, the father was said to have ignored an important moral duty towards her. It was strongly believed that parents or guardians of a girl who did not marry before puberty would certainly go to hell, so sinful was such negligence. Child marriages used to be popular and they are still in parts of Nepal.

Even more surprising is a marriage custom among the Tharus of Nepal. They arrange marriages long before the candidates for marriage are even born. This custom is known as 'marrying embryo'. In such a marriage, two pregnant women establish marriage formalities for their unborn children, assuming that they will be born of different sexes. If it happens that the children are of the same sex the 'embryo marriage' is regarded as invalid.

Equally fascinating is the custom practised among some Aborigines of Australia and among the Yanomamo people of South America. In this marriage form the father promises his baby daughter as the wife of a given adult man before she is born. It is not known when the husband commences his sexual relations with the girl.

Among the Kadar of northern Nigeria most marriages are arranged by the father when his daughter is between three and six years old. But a girl married at this age is not allowed to live with her husband for about another ten years. When the girl is older, she is free to engage in sexual relations with any man of her choice until the ten-year period lapses. She may even get pregnant and conceive the child of a lover during her time of freedom from her first husband This is not a problem, however, because the Kadar people do not cherish premarital chastity. Her early pregnancy is welcomed by her husband because it is the best proof of her fertility.

It is not always a very young girl who marries an adult male, though. For example, among some of the people of the Caucasus in Russia, there was a custom that a very small boy should marry an adult woman. The boy had to wait until he was mature to have any sexual relations with his 'old' wife. In order not to leave the newly-wed wife without a lover, a clever arrangement was made. The boy's father acted as husband to the wife. The problem of potential offspring from this relationship was solved, too. All the children from the relationship belonged to the son. The father of the married boy was said to be merely 'the seed raiser' for his son, only contributing to the building of his son's family.

Python's Wives

A peculiar cult once evolved in West Africa. Members used to venerate the python. This cult was so common in West African countries that special temples in honour of pythons were erected.

The python god was believed to be fond of beautiful women and a kind of temple prostitution developed in his temples. To become a bride of the python god a young girl had to undergo a long initiation in the temple that lasted some three years.

During this time her duty was to make love to the temple priests and worshippers. She could engage in sex with any man of her choice during the 'training' period. The girls were regarded as the python god's brides. But when they completed their course and become the god's wives they were obliged to become prostitutes, serving only the devotees of the particular temple. Any children born of these temporary relations were regarded as the children of the python god himself. Being wives of the god these women were not allowed to marry, but the temple prostitutes were admired by the community.

Many sacred pythons wandered the streets of towns. If a man encountered a python on his travels, he would bow down before it and greet it as 'My father'.

Pythons were so venerated in many parts of West Africa that even the accidental killing of one was regarded as a great offence, inviting severe punishment. Deliberate killing of pythons was revenged by torture and burning at the stake.

Temples of the sacred python were regularly visited by local people, especially the sick or crippled, who tried to reach the python god to ask him for miraculous recovery.

Worship of the python god survived in some places till the 1960s.

Woman with Many Husbands

While it is a common practice in many societies for a man to marry several women, in some societies it is women who are allowed to have more than one husband. For instance, among the Sherpas, a Buddhist people of Nepal, a girl usually marries two or more brothers. This arrangement, they say, prevents breaking up of inherited lands, and promotes solidarity among brothers who share one wife. This system of marriage could cause problems with the sexual relations of the household, but no such problem exists. The wife sleeps separately in a large bed and each husband has a separate sleeping place. They decide peacefully among themselves who will join their wife in her bedroom each night.

The custom of a woman having one or more husband is also common in parts of Brazil. Among the tribe of Aweikoma (which belongs to southern Ge) a wife can have more than one husband. The marriage is usually arranged not by the wife but by her husband.

When a man learns that his wife has a lover, he does not consider it to be an insult, but a situation which requires his action. He invites the wife's lover to accompany him on a hunting expedition. After they return from the expedition the lover moves into the couple's hut and becomes an official co-husband.

If, because of advanced age or physical weakness, the husband has difficulty supporting his family a second husband can also join the family. The first husband himself invites the younger man to become his wife's second husband. The marriage is simple if the chosen man is unmarried. If he has a wife then his wife and children must be invited as well. And the other woman becomes the wife of both men.

A fascinating variation of these practices occurs among the Nair people of Kerala in Southern India.

A young girl officially marries in a ceremony resembling a typical Hindu wedding. But the bridegroom becomes her husband for only three days; then he must divorce her and leave the house for ever.

The divorced woman is now free to have as many lovers as she desires. They are regarded as temporary husbands. She lives alone but is regularly visited by men who come at dusk and leave at dawn. A man may become her husband for ten days or more, and during this time she treats him as a real husband; she serves his sexual needs, cooks for him and washes his clothes. In exchange, her temporary husband offers her gifts or brings money.

These peculiar relationships are however very fragile and can be broken at any time by either party. The woman easily dismisses her temporary husband by simply returning his last gift.

This strange marriage system invented by Nair society seems to be ideal for promiscuous people as it provides optimum freedom for both partners. This system has no counterpart in other regions of the world.

Hostile Partners

It is often assumed that the reason for marriage is not just sexual gratification and procreation but at least mutual friendship if not love. But this is not always the case. In some cultures, even in those where monogamy is strictly observed, marriage is viewed only as a means of love-making and generating offspring. In some countries the husband and wife were virtual strangers who knew next to nothing about each other. Among the southern Slavs, girls were given to men whom they had never seen before. As G. Sumner noted in 1906: 'She comes into a strange house where . . . she is forbidden by custom to approach her husband freely, she scarcely sees him during the day; yet she may freely converse with his brothers, who were her bride attendants. The elder brother, if he is already married, and if he is polite to her, becomes her best friend'.

The marriage ceremony was not a joyful celebration in these regions and usually was a sad event for both partners. It was the custom that during the wedding the groom should neither eat nor, talk 'out of shame' and the bride had to 'weep while being dressed'.

Similar hostility among marriage partners was customary among the Cherkess of the Caucasus in Russia. A wife was ashamed to talk to her husband during the day, so any conversation was only carried out under the cover of night. A husband did not enter his wife's room by day as it was considered improper behaviour. In fact it was improper for the married couple to be seen together outside their house or to be seen talking to each other.

Similar customs were strictly observed in some regions of the South Pacific. For example, in some regions of Melanesia and Polynesia the husband had virtually no contact with his wife except during the night. They led separate lives. Married women had separate lodgings and they ate and worked separately from their husbands. Even the property of the wife and husband was kept separate.

False Couple

In some regions it is feared that evil spirits may destroy the happiness of those who are about to be married. To prevent this, various, often strange, precautions are taken to fool the evil forces.

In Southern India, it was customary on the fourth day of a wedding ceremony for a bride to disguise herself in boy's clothing and to parade in the street to deceive the evil spirits who would be unable to recognise her. It was also customary for one of the friends of the groom to become a 'false' groom but to behave like the real one, insulting the real groom and treating him as his servant or even accusing him of theft. Similar customs were also known in the past in Denmark, Israel and Morocco.

Another way of deceiving the evil spirits during a marriage ceremony was to substitute for the real couple a false couple. They would attract the attention of any evil forces and the real pair would be spared. This is the custom in a number of regions; for example in Somalia it is very common.

In Somalia the false couple are married in the house while the real couple stay in the nuptial chamber to deceive the evil spirits. The false couple may exchange their clothes and dress to impersonate the other sex. As one author notes: 'The girls dress up their partners, using padding to make the disguise as complete as possible. Then, assuming all the airs of husbands, they flog their partners with horsewhips and order them about in the same way as they themselves have been treated by young men . . .' These activities may last for a week. Those who impersonate the real couple to rescue them from the attacks of evil forces are paid well for their service.

Among the Slavs and some people of Western Europe different tricks were performed in the past to fool evil spirits during a wedding. It was customary that when the groom asked for his bride to be given to him, a false bride was provided. It could be an old woman, or a very young girl or even a man disguised as a woman.

Lending Wives

In the Muslim world a man can marry up to four wives, but his pleasure can be further extended by another type of marriage: a temporary union.

Before the birth of the prophet Mohammed, Arabs recognised a special kind of marriage which was based on a temporary contract. Although this form of marriage is now forbidden among the vast majority of Muslims, the Shi'ites consider it lawful. Such marriages are known still to take place in Iraq and Iran. In fact, even Ayatollah Khomeini taught that such marriages, even for just ten days, are often the best solution for university students.

In Iraq in the 1970s the authors were told about the existence of temporary marriages called mu'ta, which means 'rejoicing' or 'marriage for pleasure'. These marriages are officially sanctioned between a husband of the woman and another man who is obliged to pay for his 'pleasure' to the wife's 'owner'. In this case a contract is officially signed for a specific period of time. It could be for a year, several months or it could be just a marriage for one night. Strict regulations are involved and there is no right of inheritance for either party. If children are born to the 'lent' wife, they are considered legitimate and they have the right to inherit in the normal way. In the case of this temporary marriage the temporary husband has no power to divorce the woman at will. The union is simply dissolved at the end of the stipulated period. It can also be dissolved at any time by mutual consent.

Shi'ite Muslims consider such a marriage as a normal contract and although money is involved it is not called an act of prostitution but just a normal marriage.

Sunni Muslims, who do not accept mu'ta, argue that though Mohammed initially was in favour of such temporary marriages he later forbade them.

Although the utilitarian approach of Shi'ite Muslims to the problem of sexual relations seems to be unique, such a custom was reported to have existed in the past among other peoples.

12.

Bizarre Gods

Goddess of the Toilet

The Chinese had a goddess of latrines. This peculiar diety (Tzu-ku Shen) was only venerated by women, never by men. The origin of the unique cult can be traced back to the reign of the Empress Wu Hou (AD 684-705) when an educated young lady called Mei Li-ch'ing had become the concubine of an important district official. He was a married man and his wife became so jealous that she attacked the concubine in a latrine and murdered her. When the Heavenly Emperor learned of this event he decided to make the woman the goddess of latrines.

On the anniversary of her death special celebrations were performed in latrines and pigsties by country women who brought as their offerings to the goddess images of herself. The images were made from ladles. The bowl served as a head on which a human face was drawn. Willow branches were attached to the handle to make a body. The resulting image of the deity was dressed with a few rags. Incense was burnt while the assembled women asked the goddess to appear, saying: 'Your husband is away, the legitimate wife has disappeared, Little Dame, you may come out!' (Little Dame was a polite title for a wife of the second rank.) If a medium was present among the women she went into a trance and it was believed that the goddess herself was present. She was then asked through the medium about various events of the future, such as the harvest for the next year, marriages and so on.

The Japanese also had a deity of the toilet (benjo-gami) who was among the three major domestic deities associated directly with the house itself. It was said that the toilet god was asked by his believers to protect them from bladder trouble.

Tapeworm Deity

Some people in Japan used to have strange beliefs associated with the tapeworm. They believed that there is a certain deity called Amanjaka occurring in the form of a tapeworm and dwelling temporarily in a human body. Only on certain nights of the year could it invade, and only when a person was asleep. On that night, called a Koshin Night, it was believed that the tapeworm could also sneak out from a human body and send to the celestial god a report on the sins of the people inside which it had stayed. The tapeworm deity tended to present unfavourable reports to the god, even if the facts were otherwise.

To prevent this, people tried to stay awake for the whole Koshin Night. They did not allow even babies to fall asleep during the night so as not to give the tapeworm deity a chance to enter or leave.

Since it was only on this one night that Amanjaka could deliver its report, people gathered in the evening to honour the deity. They made various offerings such as food and drink to keep it busy. They assumed that after the deity indulged itself it would be too lazy to deliver a report to heaven. It was also believed that if a person avoided sleep for seven consecutive Koshin Nights he would be immune to this dangerous deity for the rest of his life.

Sexual intercourse was strictly forbidden during Koshin Night. It was believed that if a child was born as a result of love-making at this time, he would become an evil adult.

Koshin Day was an especially important event among the Japanese aristocracy. In the nineteenth century, ladies and palace officials held a special celebration during which poems composed in honour of the tapeworm deity were recited.

Living Goddess

In Nepal, visitors can witness the worship of the living goddesses known as Kumaris. There are nine Kumaris in the Kathmandu Valley. The most important and famous is the Royal Kumari. She is said to hold the power of the Kingdom of Nepal in her hands. No Nepalese king has ruled without her blessing since the eighteenth century.

The Royal Kumari is not born a goddess and she does not remain divine throughout her life. She becomes a living goddess when she is about five years old. The virgin girl is usually selected from a caste of goldsmiths. The choice is made by a special selection committee consisting of the Chief Royal Priest, several other priests and an astrologer. The girl is chosen on the basis of thirty-two qualities. Important among them are perfect health, no smallpox scars, skin without blemish and no loss of teeth. The astrologer makes sure that the girl's horoscope does not conflict with that of the ruling king.

The girl must be of strong character. She must be both fearless and sedate. Fearlessness is checked by locking about ten potential Kumaris in a dark room, where there are scary-looking masks and freshly slaughtered buffalo heads to frighten the girls. As well, eerie noises are heard. The girl who shows least fear is chosen to be the Living Goddess of Kathmandu—the Royal Kumari.

Before her final installation, several buffaloes, goats, sheep, ducks and chickens are sacrificed in front of the girl. She is beautifully dressed and her forehead is 'decorated' with the so-called third eye. She wears red clothes, her toes are painted red and she is adorned with valuable jewellery. A long white cloth is laid between the public square and the Kumari residence for the girl to ceremonially walk to her temple.

Every day the Royal Kumari sits for some three hours on her throne to receive visitors who worship her. Only about twelve people a day are allowed to visit the living goddess. As she is often still only a small child the living goddess sometimes refuses to perform her religious duty and the devotees must wait patiently until she changes her mood.

The Royal Kumari stays inside the temple during her 'appointment' which may last several years. Throughout this period she does not attend school. She remains in the high position of goddess until she sheds her first blood. This is usually the result of menstruation, but it can even be caused by an accidental cut or scratch. Once her attendant finds out that the girl has lost even one drop of blood, the king is immediately informed. It is declared that the girl has lost her divine power because the goddess has left her body. She immediately loses her great privileges and reverts to being an ordinary human being. She returns the precious jewellery to her attendants and leaves the temple for ever.

She usually leads a modest life from then on, and nobody is

interested in her fate any more. Some ex-Kumaris are even known to live in poverty. One author describing the home of a former Kumari said: 'There are no chairs, so the ex-goddess sits on the window sill of her small room, unfurnished but for a few grass mats scattered on the green-and-white linoleum. A single naked light bulb hangs from the low ceiling; fading blue paint chips from the walls. There is a broken radio, a tattered stool, and a clock with broken hands'. And the former living goddess usually remains single for the rest of her life. There is a superstition that any man who marries her would not live long.

Peasant as a God

Some people believe that divine spirits may enter human beings, permanently or temporarily. In some regions of Cambodia, it was believed that epidemics could be prevented by a god entering the body of one of the local men. Therefore, it was necessary to find the man. The people in procession went from one village to another with a band of musicians. When the man-become-god was found, he was installed at the altar of the temple. He became an object of veneration even though he had often been only a poor peasant before. The people prayed to this god-man in the belief that he could avert the plague.

Sometimes, when a divine spirit entered the body of a man, he became their god and their king. In the Marquesas Islands there was always a so-called god-man who was supposed to wield supernatural powers. Missionaries reported in the past that on each of the islands there was at least one such god-man and his position was often hereditary. According to one description, he was an old man who lived in a special temple-like house with an altar. A human skeleton hung upside down in front of it. All the surrounding trees were decorated with human skeletons.

The god inhabiting a human body among the Aztecs or Incas demanded human sacrifice. The god-man received regular human offerings, and occasionally he wished for extra sacrificial victims. Then, he simply called and his servants immediately brought him two or three victims at a time to be killed in his honour. The people believed that if the wish of their man-god was not fulfilled, he would be offended and cause a calamity. Human gods inspired so much terror that they received more human victims than all the other gods combined.

Sometimes a ruling king was defied by his people during his lifetime. For example, the Zimbas of South-east Africa worshipped only one god and he was their king. This king-god was said to govern the sky and if the rain did not stop when he wished, he used to shoot arrows at the sky to punish it for disobeying him.

Sometimes a ruling king who becomes very powerful decides to deify himself. Such was the case with the Burmese king Badonsachen, who became 'famous' for his bloodthirsty rule. More of his own people were executed than were killed in battle.

One day, the story says, the king laid aside his title, and pronounced himself a god. He left his royal palace and harem, and moved to the largest pagoda in the country. But when he tried to persuade the monks that he was the new Buddha, they became infuriated and started to demonstrate against his self-deification. The greatly disappointed king gave up his claim and returned to his palace.

Some kings were treated by the people as though they were gods. There is a tradition in Thailand that whenever the king passes, the people show their respect by prostrating themselves. When his subjects come to his court they approach his majesty on their knees with elbows resting on the ground. Even today, when ministers have an audience with the king they are obliged to 'walk' on their knees.

In the past the king was regarded as sacred. The respect was so great that the word for the king was the one which was only reserved for gods, and when Christian missionaries wanted to speak about God they had to use the Thai word for king.

So great was the respect that when talking about the king a special language had to be employed. The king's hair, hands or feet and every other part of his body had a special name. When describing the king's behaviour such as walking, sleeping or drinking, special words had to be used which must never be used to describe the actions of ordinary men.

Ruler of Gods

The Japanese emperor was for a long time regarded as a god. He was not just one among many either. He was one of the most important and powerful Shinto gods. He was an incarnation of the sun goddess who is said to rule all men and all the gods and the entire universe.

Each year for one month the king was the most important god. The month was called 'without gods'. During this time all the temples were deserted by the people since it was claimed that the gods were absent. During this month all eight hundred gods were believed to be in the king's court and serving him. The king then became the ruler of gods.

There were a number of things the emperor could not do as he was a god. He could not touch the ground with his feet, so he was carried on men's shoulders; open air was regarded as harmful to him and the sun was not worthy to shine on his head.

All parts of his body were holy so he could not cut his hair, beard and nails. 'However, lest he should grow too dirty, they may clean him in the night when he is asleep, because, they say, that which is taken from his body at that time, hath been stolen from him, and that such a theft doth not prejudice his holiness or dignity'.

The life of a god-emperor was not easy in ancient times. Every morning, he had to sit on the throne for a few hours 'Like a statue, without stirring either hands or feet, head or eyes, nor indeed any part of his body. By this means, it was thought that he could preserve peace and tranquillity in his empire. For if, unfortunately, he turned himself on one side or the other, or if he looked a good while towards any part of his dominions, it was apprehended that war, famine, fire, or some other great misfortune was near at hand to desolate the country'.

Whenever the god king had a meal, it was always from new dishes. The old ones had to be broken because it was believed that if a man ate from these sacred plates they would inflame his mouth and throat.

The emperor officially ceased to be a god in 1946 when forced to do so by the Americans. He is now, however, the 'pope' of Shinto.

God of the Kitchen

One of the most unusual Chinese gods is Zao Jun Shen, the kitchen god. His picture can be seen in traditional Chinese households. He is shown as an old man dressed in mandarin costume, with a white beard. The kitchen god is believed to reside always in the kitchen because that is the best place to observe the behaviour of each member of the family.

Believers claim that this god is busy registering on his secret list all the deeds of each family member throughout the whole year. Good and bad actions of everybody are recorded. At the end of the year the list is presented by the kitchen god in heaven. The principal god responds by decreasing or increasing the happiness of each family, depending on the people's recorded acts.

The annual trip of the kitchen god to heaven takes place on the eve of Chinese New Year. Before the god's departure each family tries to ensure that the kitchen god will report mainly their good deeds to the jade emperor in heaven.

At this time Chinese people offer their kitchen god gifts at his altar such as incense, candy and wine. During prayers they beseech the god: 'When you go to heaven you should report only good things and when you come down from heaven you should protect us and bring peace and safety to us'.

They fill the empty cup located beside his shrine with wine in the belief that the god will behave like a mortal and drink it before his departure; they expect that a bibulous god is more likely to forget the bad deeds of the people and that his report in heaven will be more favourable.

In some villages it is customary to smear the lips of the god's picture with honey so that his words about the family in heaven will be 'sweet'.

When the kitchen god is absent, his image on the home altar is turned to the wall. In some villages the god's images are burned when the god is away in heaven and when he is due to return a new image is put up.

Apart from this popular god of the kitchen, each profession in China has its own favourite god. Sometimes the same god is seen at home altars or in offices of very different professions. For example, the same god can be seen in police stations as in brothels.

Each family chooses for their altar the god who is deemed to be the most reliable. But if the god fails to help a person despite prolonged prayers and veneration, his effigy may be removed and replaced by another who it is hoped will do the job better.

Killing the God

Ancient Mexico is famous for its customs of human sacrifice. The people who were sacrificed were not always despised by the community though. Aztecs believed that some of their gods required that a person to be sacrificed should be venerated before his death;

such a person was to represent the god to whom he would be sacrificed. For a whole year, the person had to live among the people and be treated as if he were a god.

This is the story of human sacrifice to Tezcatlipoca, the powerful Aztec god of the sun. The man selected to be a human god had to be a person of unblemished body, 'slim as a reed and straight as a pillar, neither too tall nor too short'. The man was not chosen from the Aztecs themselves, but from young prisoners of war. He was decorated in a most lavish way, and as Sir James Frazer notes: 'Golden ornaments hung from his nose, golden armlets adorned his arms, golden bells jingled on his legs at every step he took'.

For the whole year this human god lived in the great luxury of the temple devoted to the god he had to personify. He was paid homage by everyone, including the nobles who served him meals as his servants. When he went through the streets he was worshipped by the people as a real god. The people threw themselves on the ground and prayed to him, asking him to cure them or to give them his blessings. As Frazer notes: 'People prayed to him with sighs and tears, taking up the dust in their hands and putting it in their mouths in token of the deepest humiliation and subjection'. And yet this same man was later brutally slain.

The temporary god was treated with great reverence by all, but he was aware that his 'divine' life was to end one day and that he would be killed by the same people who now adored him. The temporary god was always accompanied by a few servants who he knew would prevent him from escaping, if he were to attempt it.

Some twenty days before the fatal day, his life was even more improved as he was provided with four beautiful girls who became his temporary wives. These girls represented four goddesses, the goddess of the young maize, the goddess of flowers, the goddess 'our mother among the water' and the goddess of salt.

When the fatal day arrived the man had to say farewell to his beautiful wives, he was transported in a canoe across the lake to the temple of the sun god, a tall pyramid-like temple with many steps leading to its summit. The man climbed the stairs. At every step he had to break one of the flutes he had played when he represented the god of the sun. Finally he reached the summit of the temple. Several ceremonial priests were waiting for him. He was immediately seized by the priests, placed on the table and one of the priests cut open his breast and removed his still palpitating heart. The heart was then presented to the sun god. The ceremony of sacrifice was watched by the crowd surrounding the temple.

Almost as soon as the heart had stopped beating, the high priest of the temple announced the name of the next sacrificial victim, to be killed after twelve months.

Sacrifice to the Fire God

Among the ritual sacrifices performed by the ancient Maya and Aztecs the most unusual seems to have been in honour of the earth goddess Teteoinnan. This important Aztec deity was responsible for the harvest and was the most demanding of gods. To please her it was customary to slay at her altar not one human victim but five at once. The first victim had to be a woman. After ritual killing, her body was flayed by one of the priests. One portion of skin from the victim's thigh was then used to cover the face of one of the high priests who served another god, the maize harvest god called Cinteotl. The rest of her skin was used by the young man selected to personify the Earth Goddess.

Escorted by ceremonial priests the man disguised in human skin entered the goddess's temple where he sacrificed four more persons waiting there.

Certain gods were believed to demand extremely cruel tortures of the sacrificial victims before they were put to death. For example, to satisfy the god of fire Xuihtecuthli a newly-wed young couple had to be chosen. The priests had to select a most handsome recently married couple. On the fatal day a huge fire was lit near the altar of the god of fire. Then at a given signal the ceremonially dressed couple were thrown live into the flames. The priest's assistants carefully observed their ordeal and when the victims were about to die they raked them out of the flame. Their breasts were then cut open, their still palpitating hearts removed and offered as a gift to the demanding god.

Sacred Cactus

Zacatec Indians of Mexico had the custom that when a boy was born his father had to undertake a special test of endurance. The man had to sit and bear incredible torture inflicted by his friends. While he sat the men inserted weapons of torture into his body. Their weapons were sharp teeth or bones. As a result of his friends' actions his whole body was punctured, resulting in severe blood loss. The purpose of this weird custom was to examine the endurance of the boy's father. This indicated how courageous his son would be when he grew up. The father could bear the pain because he was under the influence of an intoxicating cactus called peyote which he consumed just before the ceremony.

This modest-looking plant is regarded by Mexican Indians as the greatest gift of the gods. The small spineless cactus has powerful hallucinogenic properties; when eaten it produces such remarkable well-being and sensations that it is regarded as a glimpse of paradise. Vivid coloured images of unknown fantastic worlds are so powerful that a person may believe that he is having contact with the gods. Some people even experience a feeling of being weightless during their intoxication.

No wonder this plant became an object of worship. A special religious cult evolved among the Indian tribes in which peyote became a kind of holy sacrament. Already in the 1890s more than fifty Indian tribes north of the Rio Grande were members of the peyote cult. To prevent the use of the habit-forming peyote American authorities tried to suppress its use. But all their efforts were in vain because the devotees of the strange cult used the sacred plant in secret. The cult was finally legalised and the Native American Church was formed for peyote users in 1918.

The cult members now call themselves Christians despite the fact that their great spirit is still peyote which is used as a kind of holy communion. They do believe in Christ but claim that he was only one of the great spirits sent to the earth by God.

In some regions peyote has become a panacea for any ailment. Some people even believe that it can cure blindness. The local shaman usually demonstrates his incredible power to forecast the future, to find lost property or even to produce rain when he is in a trance after using peyote.

Peyote has such an enormous value to many Indian tribes that they make long trips to gather it. Mexican Huichol Indians, who are addicted to peyote, make pilgrimages on foot up to 300 miles. During a trip to the desert where the cactus grows the men have no food except the cactus itself. Their pilgrimage is usually led by the local shaman. He is the first to see the precious cactus growing among the rocks. Before it is collected, he shoots an arrow from his bow in order to prevent the spirit inhabiting the plant from escaping.

After gathering peyote, the Indians usually return so exhausted that they are almost unrecognisable, but they are happy as they have a supply of the magic plant for the whole year.

Sacred Bear

The Ainu people of Japan are famous for their incredible customs and beliefs. They are not ethnic Japanese but they live on several islands belonging to Japan.

Their religion was based on worship of a bear. The same animal was hunted by the Ainu and their subsistence was based on it. The Ainu believed that a giant bear came from the sky and rescued their people during a great famine. To commemorate this important event, a special ceremony is organised. In this celebration, which lasts for three days every spring, the main role was played by the bear.

This celebration was most cruel as during the ceremony the bear was tortured to death. It was usually a young bear, especially reared for this purpose. If the bear was captured very young, it was suckled by the women of the village.

On a special day the bear was led in procession to a holy place where the great offering to the gods was to be made. When the people assembled in front of the cage, a specially chosen man addressed the bear in a manner prescribed by tradition.

An example of such a speech is given by an eyewitness: 'O thou divine one, thou wast sent into the world for us to hunt. O thou precious little divinity, we worship thee; pray hear our prayer. We have nourished thee and brought thee up with a deal of pains and trouble, all because we love thee so . . . Now we are about to send thee to thy father and mother'.

After the speech the bear was released from the cage and tethered to a pole. Then it was bombarded with a lot of blunt arrows in order to excite the animal but not to kill it. Finally, the furious bear was shot at by an elderly man with a normal sharp arrow. The animal's head was tethered to two poles and the animal was then strangled to death by many people. The head of the sacrificed animal was cut off and set on a long pole in the belief that the spirit of the bear will travel more easily to the sky. The remaining parts of the bear's flesh were cooked and eaten by all who participated in the celebration during a great feast which followed.

The first account of this strange bear festival was provided by a Japanese writer in 1652. In his book he described the way in which the sacrificial bear was 'squeezed to death' by fifty to sixty people, Ainu men and women. But despite the fact that the animal was tortured the executioners did not forget to ask for its forgiveness and favour before it died. 'You will ask God to send us, for the winter, plenty of otters and sables, and for summer, seals and fish in abundance. Do not forget our messages, we love you much, and our children will never forget you'.

Among various customs practised by the Ainu people, probably the most famous was female tattooing. A broad blue tattoo was made around the mouth of a young girl and was later improved in stages over a period of several years to make the girl more attractive as a marriage partner. From a distance a tattooed girl looked as if she had a moustache. As the tattooing was a painful operation, the Japanese decided to prohibit the custom by law. However, some old women in the villages can still be seen with this peculiar decoration around their mouths.

Bloodthirsty Goddess

Among the Hindu deities the most cruel and vindictive is the goddess Kali. She is the goddess of death and destruction, responsible for plague, cholera, smallpox and other calamities. She is traditionally portrayed as a naked black woman with four hands. While two of her hands are raised in a gesture of blessing, in the third she holds a severed human head dripping blood and in the fourth a sword or a rope showing her desire for killing. Her body is adorned with a necklace of human skulls. Even her earrings are made of baby skulls.

Small wonder that human sacrifice was considered to be the only way to propitiate this frightening goddess. Annual ceremonies of human sacrifice were seen as recently as the early nineteenth century, especially in north-eastern India.

It was usually a volunteer who was sacrificed in the honour of the goddess. It was an important event and the execution was watched by crowds of people. The victim, beautifully dressed for the occasion, was placed on a specially erected platform so that everybody could see the sacrifice. As the sacrifice was a voluntary act of one of the worshippers, the executioner had to wait until the victim had made a sign that he was ready to die. The head of the victim was severed and then ritually offered to the goddess on a golden plate. It was also the custom of some yogis to eat the cooked lung of a sacrificial victim. The victim's blood mixed with rice was also ceremonially eaten by some local rajahs and his family members.

In more recent years only an occasional human sacrifice was made, but in the sixteenth century there were mass sacrifices. For example, in 1565 a rajah named Nara Narayama was such an admirer of the bloodthirsty goddess that he offered her 740 severed heads of his people. The heads were presented, the story says, on copper plates in a temple in Assam devoted to this goddess.

As late as 1830, one rajah slew twenty-five adult men as a sacrifice to the demanding goddess. The British officially prohibited this cruel custom in 1832.

Although it is believed that it has been completely eradicated, some fanatical Hindu sect members still hold the belief that only human blood can appease the demanding goddess. Reports of human sacrifice still crop up from time to time in the Indian press, although they are rare. On 17 March 1980 a ritual human sacrifice was reported by the *Times* of India. According to this report a 32-year-old man had taken his daughter into a local village temple and slit her throat, offering her to the goddess Kali. In another report published in the *Indian Express* one father slew with an axe his four children who were all under seven years old. This horrific act was said to have been performed in front of the image of the goddess.

13.
Incredible Faiths

Devil Worshippers

Most of us see the Devil or Satan as a horrible creature with cloven hoofs and a forked tail. But such a description is unacceptable to the Yezidis, a Kurdish religious sect. They number some 50,000 and live in secluded valleys of Northern Iraq and Turkey. They worship the Devil as the chief angel. They believe he rules the world on behalf of God. They say that it is not God but Satan who should be worshipped. God they say is benevolent, and does not need to be worshipped. But Satan is actively malevolent so it is wise 'to bestow special care in propitiating the Devil'.

The Yezidis believe that Satan was among the chief angels and was expelled from heaven by God because of his rebellious pride. God, however, forgave him when he repented and made him the ruler of the whole world. Yezidis believe that the fallen angel punishes those people who annoy him even unintentionally by just pronouncing his name. The utterance of the word Satan or even words which sound similar may offend the fallen angel.

Fear of the word Satan is so strong that even hearing such 'dangerous' words uttered by non-believers had to be avoided. This taboo occasionally benefited Yezidis, though. In 1872, some young Yezidis refused to serve in the Turkish army; in their petition for exemption they explained that they would not be able to avoid hearing the word Satan used by other, non-Yezidi, soldiers. Every Muslim, they claimed, was accustomed to saying 'Take refuge with Allah from Shaitan ar-eashim (Satan the Stoned)'. When a Yezidi soldier heard the phrase, disrespectful of their fallen angel, he would have to kill his comrade or commit suicide.

A Fulani man during a beauty contest.

Initiation ceremony among Mandans of North America.

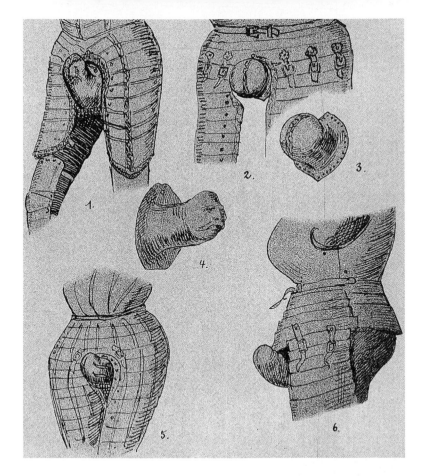

Sixteenth century codpieces in armour.

A phallic image
of a deity in the
Japanese countryside.

Phallic brow ornament
(southern Ethiopia).

A shrunken head of
the Jivaros (Ecuador).

The Living Goddess
of Nepal.

'Giraffe-necked' Padaung woman (Burma).

Aboriginal witch doctor of Northern Territory.

Mudmen from Asaro Valley of Papua New Guinea.

An image of the goddess Kali.

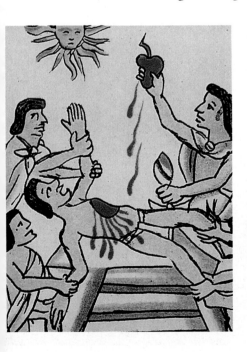

Aztec human sacrifice.

Phallic procession at
Tagata shrine in Japan.

Penile sheath of a Dani man of Irian Jaya.

As the name Satan is taboo, Yezidis use for Satan the Kurdish name of the peacock angel which is Malek Ta'us. The effigy of the Malek Ta'us is made of iron or bronze. It represents a standing peacock. The effigy weighs up to 300 kg. Most of the time much smaller effigies are used.

During religious celebrations the peacock angel effigy is carried by special priests from village to village. The priest sends his assistant on horseback to inform people of his arrival. The effigy is uncovered as the people sing hymns. The priest gradually enters a trance which is so deep that finally his 'head drops near the bird'. In total silence he soon recovers consciousness and then informs the devotees that the spirit of Malek Ta'us has entered the sacred effigy. In response to this statement all present kneel and kiss the image and place gifts on a special plate.

The most famous shrine of this unusual faith is located in a secluded valley of Mount Lalish some sixty miles from Mosul in northern Iraq. The authors visited this unusual shrine in 1973. On the entrance door we noticed the large black figure of a serpent engraved. It was kissed by the devotees before they entered the shrine. They jump over a large stone door sill. It should never be touched as it is the place where the sun's rays first hit in the morning. Inside, the walls were black. There were no windows but small oil lamps lit up the tomb of Sheikh Adi, the Yezidis' saint and sect founder. The tomb resembled a four-poster bed and was covered with a red and green cloth. A special inscription on the wall was an invocation of the mercy of the Malek Ta'us. It was so dark inside that the shrine obviously had to be dedicated to the King of Darkness.

Yezidis impose a strict taboo on the colour blue. The reason is that the Heaven from which the fallen angel was expelled is blue and the colour is disliked by Satan.

The Yezidis have two religious books. One is called the Black Book because all words resembling the word Satan are blacked out. In this book the Malek Ta'us speaks to his people in the first person and promises rewards to those who worship him and punishment to those who offend him.

This unusual faith attracted the attention of Hitler who is said to have become interested in the sacred Yezidi books before World War II. He sent special emissaries to steal some secret Yezidi manuscripts. The sacred books, however, were too well guarded. Some claim that Hitler hoped to find in this incredible faith an additional new magic weapon in his efforts to conquer the world.

People from Another Planet

In certain regions of the world in the past, some people had strange shaped heads. Some were incredibly elongated. These people could have come from another planet. But this peculiar shaped skull was the result of deliberate human intervention.

Among the ancient Maya this was done so that people's heads would resemble the skull of the jaguar.

The ancient Maya venerated the jaguar so much that they tried to do everything possible to resemble the sacred beast. Because the jaguar has a flattened skull, parents deformed the heads of their infants by binding special boards around the baby's skull. The technique was effective because human heads can change shape by manipulating the skull in infancy and during the first few years of life. The desired shape can be accomplished by applying gentle but continuous pressure. This is possible because at such an early age the child's skull is soft and malleable.

Deformation of human skulls was not confined to the ancient Maya civilisation. In Egypt, Cyprus and Crete (from the second millennium) it was also practised. Only women of high birth who were members of the ruling dynasties, had the privilege of having a deformed head.

The practice of deforming the human skull was still widespread in the Middle Ages and in certain regions of Europe till fairly modern times. This was accomplished by 'flattening the crown by means of cords and tight caps'. This practice was still widespread in the 1920s on the islands of Marken in the Zuider Zee (former inlet of North Sea).

Deformation of human skulls was practised until recent times in Patagonia (Argentina) and Greenland.

Deformation of the human head was practised in Nazi Germany where some parents tried to deform the heads of their infants in the belief that the racially despised round head would be changed into the most favoured elongated head of the so called 'master race'.

In some cultures there was a custom of performing a drastic intervention in the skull of a living person by cutting off and removing roundels of bone from the brain case. Such operations are said to be still occasionally performed in Bolivia. The roundels removed from the skull of a living person were said to cure the person from certain serious disease. It was also used as an amulet to ward off evil.

Cargo Cult

When the first European ship arrived in New Guinea, the impact of the visit on local people must have been more powerful than a flying saucer would be today. The people had never seen a white man before. But they had the belief that their ancestors were white. No wonder they thought these men were their ancestors, from the land of the dead. And when they saw a huge boat loaded with fabulous goods they had never seen before, it was obvious to them that these goods must have come from heaven.

Although they soon learned that white people were not their ancestors, the incredible mystery of the origin of the goods remained a puzzle to the natives. Their 'philosophers' came to the conclusion that Europeans had acquired their machines and wealth from certain mysterious and powerful spirits. Soon a kind of religious belief sprang up that became known in the West as cargo cult.

Cult leaders argued that such precious cargo could be sent down to them by spirits if they learnt how to observe certain religious rules. Some elders asserted that the cargo found in European hands had been stolen from the natives when it was delivered to them by their ancestors. When the natives became familiar with the Bible they started to accuse Europeans of having deliberately torn from all the copies the first page, where it was written that God was a Papuan.

Cult leaders maintained that the expected cargo would arrive shortly. To facilitate delivery they even started to build a kind of airstrip. Some cult leaders argued that in order to receive their cargo they must mimic the behaviour of white people. So they organised offices in their huts and exchanged worthless pieces of paper among themselves.

Some cult leaders advised people that in order to speed the arrival of the cargo all social customs had to be changed. Sexual intercourse between husband and wife was forbidden and replaced by incest.

Sometimes the exact date of the cargo delivery was predicted whereupon people began slaughtering their domestic animals and destroying all the possessions they now considered useless.

Disappointed, and still with unfulfilled desires, some people decided to become Christians. They believed that by doing so they would obtain the precious cargo. When again this did not happen and the cargo did not come, they began accusing missionaries of withholding a special prayer which they claimed could bring the cargo.

One peculiar faith based on cargo cult was born on the small island of Tanna, Vanuatu, as late as the 1940s. An American pilot named John Frum landed on this island. When he flew on, he left a great amount of wealth. Local people thought it was the long expected cargo from heaven. They started to worship the pilot, regarding him as a god.

A few years later, when a plane of the American Red Cross landed on Tanna, the people assumed that the visiting medical officer was the messenger of their god, John Frum. They took the red cross insignia which they saw on the uniform of the officer as a symbol of their new faith. They erected small crosses and surrounded them with a picket fence.

The peculiar cargo cult has never died out and some islanders have not lost their hope that John Frum will return with his cargo. In an effort to communicate with their deity, they built special towers. They strung up wires with empty tin cans and believed this to be their radio station, set to facilitate contact with their god.

Hungry Devil

A curious belief has evolved among the tin miners of the high Andes plateau in Bolivia. Constant hazards of landslides and explosions of gas make their mine extremely dangerous. Many fatal accidents occur. To ease their terror these miners decided to choose a rather strange patron, namely the devil. Although they regard themselves as Christians they believe that their mine is under the control of the devil who must be propitiated. They call him affectionately tio—uncle. They say that 'all the mineral that comes from the interior of the mine is the "crop" of the devil and whether one likes it or not, we have to invite the tio to drink and eat so that the flow of metal will continue'.

To please their patron the miners make his effigies and place them in various parts of the mine. The effigies are made of ore and have human-like faces. Bulbs from electric torches are placed in the eye sockets while the teeth are made of glass pieces. The mouth of the effigy is left open to enable the devil to smoke, eat and drink.

The miners give to the effigy various offerings such as sugar cakes, rice and coca leaves and they put a lit cigarette into his mouth in the belief that he enjoys smoking. A miner would then say: 'Tio, help us in our work. Don't let any accident happen'.

Whenever, despite this, a fatal accident takes place miners say that it was the tio who ate them because he was hungry, and that this meant the offerings were insufficient. In response a special celebration is organised during which more generous offerings are made including a sacrifice of animals. Two llamas, one male and one female are ritually slain and their hearts removed and blood collected. By adding wine and sweets these precious gifts are then put into a special hole made in the ore. The miners also cast some wine from a bottle begging the devil not to 'eat' any more of their mates.

In some corridors of the mine the figure of tio is made in a different way. It has an erect penis some 30 cm long. When a distressed worker finds himself in a state of sexual impotence, he immediately visits the figure in the belief that the tio will miraculously make him potent again.

'Good' Witches

Although we would probably associate witches solely with the past, there are still witches in the UK, USA and other western countries. Unlike the witches of the past, they are not worshippers of the devil. They claim to be 'good' witches who practise witchcraft for the benefit of humanity. They claim to be practising an ancient religion which involves the worship of two deities, namely the earth mother and the horned god. But they strongly stress that there is no connection between the horned god and the devil. To them the horned god is a fertility god whom they usually call by the Roman name of Janus. This god is responsible for weather and crops and the rituals promote fertility of the earth.

In the witches' sacred book, the earth goddess says: 'Listen to the words of the Great Mother who was of old called among men Artemis, Astarte, Diana, Melusine, Ceridwen, Arianrod, Baich and many other names . . . Whenever ye need of anything once in the month and better it be if the Moon is full then shall ye assemble in some secret place and adore Me who am Queen of all witcheries . . . I shall teach ye things unknown and ye shall be free from all slavery. As a sign that ye be really free ye shall be naked in your rites and ye shall dance, sing, feast, make love— all in Praise of Me'.

Members of this cult recognise three grades of witches and their initiation ceremony is truly incredible. The person to be initiated is stripped naked and blindfolded and then led to the so called 'circle of power'. There the leader of the group utters various occult words and the initiate is kissed on feet, knees, genitals, breast and lips. Then he receives forty strokes of the scourge. Finally the initiate takes an oath in which he states that he will never reveal the secrets of the art to anybody outside the cult.

The initiation for the second degree is similar but this time the initiate is supposed to give 120 strokes of the scourge to the initiator.

For the third degree, ritual sexual intercourse is supposed to take place between the candidate and the initiator.

Although so-called modern witches claim to be good and to have nothing to do with the devil they celebrate the same festivals as medieval witches. Details of their rituals vary from group to group. According to one report the following were the instructions given to a group of witches before their Candlemas festival: 'Procede to the site with a dance step, waving brooms and lighted torches; all, dancing, form the Magic Circle. The High Priest enters, in his right hand the consecrated Magic Sword, in his left hand a wooden image of an erect phallus. Priest and Priestess exchange the fivefold kiss (on feet, knees, genitals, breast and lips). The Priestess then invokes the god into the Priest with Invocation . . . Initiations are then held (if there are any) followed by the Cakes and Wine ceremony, the Great Rite if possible, a feast and a communal dance'. The great rite mentioned in the quote is ritual sexual intercourse between priest and priestess.

In the early 1970s there were said to be between five and ten thousand modern witches in the UK alone.

In addition, it should be stressed that there are small groups of people in the West who declare themselves to be devil worshippers. The so-called 'First Church of Satan' was established in San Francisco in 1966. The satanists have rather unusual temples because the body of a living naked girl is often placed on their altars and worshipped.

Meriah

Among the Khonds of Bengal it was not sufficient for the head of the family to witness the ceremony of human sacrifice to the goddess of earth called Tari Pennu. Every family head had to bury a piece of the flesh of the sacrificial victim in his field. Otherwise their land would not yield any crops. Human sacrifice to this goddess was practised in Bengal as late as the mid-nineteenth century.

This kind of human sacrifice was of paramount importance for turmeric because its roots required, it was said, human blood in order to acquire its deep colour.

Strangely, the goddess did not accept just any human being as a sacrifice in her honour. She demanded that the sacrificial victim (called meriah) be purchased for the event by the worshippers. Occasionally the Khonds used to sell their own children in the belief that by this sacrifice they would ensure sanctity of their spirits.

A person destined to become a sacrificial victim was often kept alive for many years before he was sacrificed. He was treated with sympathy and great respect, and was welcomed everywhere. A boy sacrifice who reached the age of marriage was given a wife and was even provided with some land to cultivate. His wife would also be assigned to sacrifice in future. According to tradition, all their children would become sacrificial victims when they grew up.

When the date of sacrifice was arranged, the victim was anointed with precious oils and decorated with flowers. He was then led in solemn procession to a special sacred grove. He was tied to a post while the surrounding crowd danced around him. They addressed to the victim the following words: 'We bought thee with a price, we did not seize thee, and now according to custom we sacrifice thee; no sin rests upon us'. Saying this the assembled people began to struggle among themselves as each tried to secure magical relics from the victim's decorations. Some people even begged the victim for a drop of his saliva so that they could anoint their heads for good luck.

Then the final execution took place. The way the meriah was put to death varied, depending upon region. The most widespread method was strangulation. In some areas, however, the death of the victim was not a simple strangulation but the result of horrific torture.

People used to cut off the victim's flesh when he was alive to secure a small portion, and then the dying victim was dragged across the fields.

One macabre method commonly used was to fasten the living victim to a wooden proboscis made like that of an elephant. While the proboscis was whirling around with the victim attached, the people cut off the pieces of the man's flesh. In some sacrifices employed by Khonds a slow death was inflicted on the victim by roasting him on a fire. It was strongly believed that the more pain inflicted during his ordeal and the more tears shed by the victim before his death the more rain would be sent by the deity and the better would be the yield of their crops.

Flesh cut off the sacrificial victim had a special value. It was immediately carried away by specially delegated people from each village. To secure rapid delivery of the flesh to the villages, special messengers ran to their respective communities at great speed. In every village the messenger carrying the flesh was received by a priest who divided it into two portions. One was offered to the earth goddess to be buried in the ground, while the other portion was divided into as many parts as there were families in the village. The flesh was then buried by the head of the family in his favoured field.

Only after prolonged efforts were the British colonial authorities eventually able to eradicate this barbaric custom, which was replaced by the sacrifice of a buffalo calf.

Sacred Pickaxe

A cruel sect evolved in India among some of the devotees of the goddess Kali. The sect members who were called Thugs believed that the goddess ordered her devotees to strangle human victims in her honour. They claimed that Kali had shown some of her devotees how to do it correctly on a clay dummy using a handkerchief. She gave them one of her curved fangs as an emblem of their religion. Afterwards, the sect worshipped the fang as the sacred pickaxe. The Thugs strangled thousands of travellers and pilgrims as offerings to the demanding goddess.

The Thugs formed small groups and operated along the pilgrim routes. They first got acquainted with a pilgrim and then accompanied him before his execution. To entertain him, they behaved in a most friendly way so that the victim suspected nothing.

While the pilgrim rested among his new 'friends', he was suddenly strangled. The Thugs acted swiftly. On a given signal, one of them slipped his scarf around the victim's neck and suffocated him to death. But the victim was not killed immediately. The noose was released for some time so that the goddess had an opportunity to watch and enjoy the victim's slow agony.

The corpse was dismembered by a specialised sect member. It was believed that the more vigorously the body was mutilated the more pleasing would it be to the goddess of destruction and terror.

The body was then buried and over the victim's grave a special ceremony was performed during which a solution of sugar called the goor, and regarded as sacred, was drunk by the murderers.

The Thugs had no compassion for those whom they betrayed and then tortured to death because they believed that such killings were their religious duty and that those who were chosen to die were preordained by the goddess herself.

The Thugs never killed women, evidently sparing them because the goddess was a woman herself, and might be offended. They also spared the blind or those whose bodies showed a natural or inflicted mutilation. For some unknown reason the Thugs also exempted from their attacks various craftsmen such as smiths, shoemakers and carpenters.

These horrific murderers normally pursued exemplary and peaceful lives. They were family men, and their double life usually remained unknown to the rest of the community. One Thug whose identity was later discovered, served for many years as a devoted nurse in a British family. Suspicion arose when it was noticed that the nurse always disappeared for a few weeks each year, explaining that he had to make a long trip to comfort his sick mother.

The Thugs became such enthusiastic killers that they never even considered changing their life style or giving up ritual killing. One Thug confessed: 'Let any man taste the goor and he will be a thug; my mother's family was opulent, her relations high in office . . . yet I was always miserable while absent from my gang, and obliged to return to Thugges . . . if I were to live a thousand years I should never be able to follow any other trade'.

As thousands of pilgrims never came home from their trips the British authorities started a long war against the Thugs. By 1837 more than 3000 sect members had been captured and over 400 were sentenced to death and hanged. The sect has ceased to exist and the last known Thug was hanged in 1882.

White Primitives

It is hard to believe, but some Christians in the United States regard the use of cars, radio, television or even electricity as evil. These restrictions are adhered to even today by the Amish, who have rejected the modern way of life and know-how and have preserved their own traditional and simple way of life.

The Amish have rejected the luxuries of contemporary civilisation and even all the modern mechanical inventions used in agriculture. As one of the Amish explained: 'Tractor gets the work done more quickly, but horses and the love of hard work keep us nearer to God'.

It is easy to recognise a member of the Amish sect as they dress in old-fashioned clothes, made in the style of around 250 years ago. They have weird restrictions about their clothing. For example, they reject buttons. They argue that buttons symbolise military uniforms, and the Amish despise war. So Amish men fasten their vests and coats with hooks and eyes, while the women fasten their aprons and capes with straight pins.

When an Amish man marries, it is customary for him to grow a beard. Moustaches, however, are not permitted.

The Amish have their own peculiar concept of education, too. Their schools are of one room and are ungraded. Amish children complete their education at the age of fourteen. After this, boys start working on the farms and the girls are supposed to lead a life of domesticity.

The Amish have been separated for centuries from the outside world and their way of life is so simple that they are sometimes called 'white primitives'. They are naturally highly religious although they do not have churches and services are conducted at home.

They despise outsiders, and glorify their religion which is an offshoot of the Mennonites. They came to America in the eighteenth century from Germany where they were being persecuted. The Amish speak their own language, a dialect of German, but largely forgotten in Germany. Their faith is based on their sacred book, *The Bloody Theatre of Martyrs* which includes numerous accounts of Christians who chose torture and death when defending their faith. This 1500 page tract is full of vivid descriptions of crucifixions, stonings and even live burials of the early Christians.

Non-violence to Plants

Although in theory, Hindus and Buddhists refrain from taking animal life, it is the Jains who carry non-violence to an extreme. The members of this Indian sect take great efforts not even accidentally to kill or harm any living beings, moving or stationary, from above or below the earth. Jain monks wear a white cloth in front of their mouths to prevent accidentally swallowing a flying insect. They also carry brooms, with which they sweep the ground before them, to avoid accidentally stepping on insects. Jains even avoid drinking water after dark because they fear that small insects may be overlooked and swallowed. They allow a mosquito to suck their blood. Similarly, pious Jains would rather suffer the bites of bedbugs than destroy them. Wealthy Jains used to employ special servants to lie in the master's bed to 'feed' the bed-bugs so that their masters could have a good rest at night.

While ordinary Jains must only avoid killing living beings, a monk's obligation of non-violence goes much further. If a monk bathes in the river he must not swim violently but he has to float as gently as possible in order not to disturb the water 'atoms', thereby extending the rule of non-violence even to non-living things.

Jain monks believe as well that 'killing' plants by cooking is a sin. A monk will wait for someone to cook the plants for him so that he can eat an already 'dead' vegetable.

Because of the non-violence principle, many jobs are closed to Jains. Working on a farm is out of the question because ploughing or hoeing involves killing insects or larvae living in the soil.

It would seem, therefore, that restrictions should have led Jains to extreme poverty but this has not been the case. Some sect members have accumulated considerable wealth as successful tradesmen and businessmen.

Although few in number, the Jains are very influential. Many are prominent in Indian political life. The Jains have built such impressive temples as the famous temple on Mount Abu, which is made of white marble and beautifully adorned with miniature towers and rich decorations.

Living Buddha

Although the Dalai Lama is so well known, few people realise that he was the God-King of Tibet. He is the incarnation of Chenrezi, the God of Grace, one of the Living Buddhas. Tibetans believe that their ancestors were born from the sexual union between Chenrezi and a female demon.

In fact all Tibetan rulers are said to be incarnations of Chenrezi. Dalai Lama is not the only Incarnation of Buddha and living god of Tibet. His eldest and youngest brothers are regarded as different incarnations of Buddha. In fact all the lamas of Tibet, numbering more than a thousand, are incarnations of previous lamas and are regarded as gods. An incarnation of a lama can also take place outside Tibet. In fact a few years ago an incarnation of a deceased lama was found in Spain. This caused considerable problems. Eventually the Spanish parents gave permission for their son to be sent to a Tibetan monastery to undergo training.

A man is identified as an incarnation when he is still a very small child. It is truly perplexing how an incarnation of a given lama could be found among the many thousands of small children. The story of the discovery of the present Dalai Lama illustrates this intricate process.

When the previous Dalai Lama died, his body was seated in state looking towards the south. One morning the monks noticed that his head was turned to the east. In order to explain this, the State Oracle was consulted, and although no explanation was provided, in a trance the monk threw a scarf in the direction of the rising sun, confirming the direction where the child incarnation lives.

For the next two years no new clues were obtained. The child could not be found, although emissaries travelled extensively. Finally, the regent who governed on behalf of the yet-to-be-found Dalai Lama, in despair decided to spend several days near a sacred lake where visions of the future could be seen. During this meditation he saw a vision of a monastery with roofs of jade green and gold and near it a small house with turquoise tiles. The excited regent informed his emissaries and they began to search for a monastery which fitted his vision.

Soon, the searching men had found a monastery which exactly matched the regent's vision. Near it there was a small house covered with turquoise tiles. Inside, they found a two year old boy. Although the emissaries were disguised, the small boy immediately recognised them and declared that he was the reincarnation of the Dalai Lama.

The messengers were still suspicious and performed a number of tests to make sure that the boy was not lying. Various objects formerly used by the late Dalai Lama together with some he had never used were placed before the boy. In every instance, the story says, the boy picked up the things used by the deceased Dalai Lama.

The messengers were finally convinced that they had discovered the new incarnation. They fell down and paid homage to the child. The great news was soon announced throughout Tibet. In great splendour, the boy-god was transported to Lhasa, where a huge crowd and foreign dignitaries were waiting to greet him as the Dalai Lama. The boy was carried on a special throne. People prostrated themselves as if he were a god. Despite being only two, the boy sat for many hours with remarkable dignity and composure.

The present, fourteenth, Dalai Lama went into exile after the Chinese occupation of Tibet. He has been residing near Dharamsala in North India. In 1989 he was awarded the Nobel Peace Prize for his constant opposition to the use of violence in the world.

Sacred Tooth

A fallen tooth or a bone would seem to be of no value whatsoever. But if a tooth, a piece of bone or even a hair can be said to have belonged to a holy man or a prophet, it may have enormous value as a religious relic. Among the most precious is the tooth of Buddha found in Sri Lanka.

The tooth has a fascinating history. It is said to have been snatched from the Buddha's funeral pyre (543 BC) and smuggled into Sri Lanka. This relic was so precious that it was usually housed in a palace more magnificent than that of a ruling king. Finally the tooth was housed in a special temple in Kandy.

When that city was captured by the Portuguese, they claimed to have captured and destroyed the precious relic because it was the symbol of the power of the whole nation. But the people claim that the Portuguese were tricked by the temple priests; they placed a false tooth in the casket, while the real one was hidden.

At present, the famous tooth is housed in the Temple of the Tooth built by Sri Wickrama Rajasinha the last king of Kandy. The tooth is housed in a heavy gold casket. There is a series of smaller and smaller caskets and the smallest in the centre is the one which contains the tooth. The casket is always guarded by two monks.

The sacred tooth is ritually maintained by an entire hierarchy of temple priests, who bathe it, clothe it and even feed it every day. The tooth is associated with miracles. In the first century BC, it is believed that the casket containing the precious tooth rose suddenly, opened itself, and the tooth came out and changed itself into Buddha who performed miracles.

A great festival in honour of the tooth is organised every year during which thousands of pilgrims come to the temple to make offerings. Even during this festival, which lasts ten days, only the casket containing the famous tooth can be seen by worshippers. The casket is carried in procession on the back of a huge elephant. The animal is beautifully dressed and ornamented in gold embroidery. Many other elephants also take part in this unusual parade.

The famous tooth of which the Sri Lankan people are so proud is not the only tooth of Buddha which survived his cremation. So many temples in East Asia claim to have a Buddha's tooth that the total would be several times the number of teeth a man can have. In Beijing alone during the Great Tang dynasty (AD 618-906) four temples claimed to house a Buddha tooth.

Paradise Before Death

The Assassins were a Muslim sect whose duty was to kill enemies as ordered by their leader. Young men were eager to join this dangerous group because they were told by the sect leader that they would immediately go to paradise if killed in action.

In order to prove his claims, Al Hasan Ibn-al-Sagah, the sect leader, gave his adherents a sample of life in paradise by a very clever arrangement. A candidate for membership was invited to the castle and given a large dose of a sleeping drug. During his sleep he was transferred to the castle's garden. It was a most extravagant garden with beautiful flowers and fruit. The food and music was the best one could imagine. Several beautiful girls in the garden were especially trained and could fulfil any sexual desires of the young candidate. For a period of five days the initiate experienced a life about which he had probably never even dreamed. To make his stay even more fantastic the candidate was given hashish. After five days, the man was transferred back to the sect leader's court.

Having experienced life in 'paradise' the candidate was happy to join the sect and ready to obey any orders of the sect leader.

One chronicle describes an incident which characterises the remarkable commitment and high morale of the assassins. One day, as a visitor to Hasan's castle was having a discussion with the sect leader on the ramparts of the famous castle in the mountains, the sect leader said: 'You see that guard on yonder turret top. When the visitor said yes, Hasan made a signal to the guard, who immediately threw up his hands in salutation and plunged 2000 feet to his death'.

The Assassins were also called Hashishins because they used hashish so often. They only used daggers in their work, although poison or arrows were much more reliable and safer to use in those days. Even after a killing, an Assassin did not attempt to escape quickly. They were often caught and found guilty and executed.

This dangerous but powerful organisation was founded by Hasan in 1090 in Persia. Its members killed hundreds of religious and political enemies, especially Sunni Muslims. The sect challenged the right of the Caliphs of Baghdad to rule the Muslim world. The sect's ferocious activity did not cease even after the death of its leader. They continued their deadly duty for over a hundred years. It was only after the siege of their castle by Mongols in 1256 that the Assassins were forced to surrender. Thousands of Assassins were massacred and that year signified the end of this cruel sect.

Indian Supermen

Hindu ascetics practise various forms of self-torture as a means of acquiring spiritual or magical power. Most Hindu ascetics observe complete abstinence from sex and in one sect, to demonstrate purity, followers wear iron rings around their penis. One method of selfmutilation involves never unclenching their fists. As a result their fingernails grow and penetrate the flesh, causing permanent pain. Another way of self-torture is chosen by certain ascetics who raise their arms and keep them in that position for so long that eventually their muscles atrophy. Some ascetics constantly look at the sky so that after a time the muscles of their neck become dysfunctional and their heads cannot move. Other ascetics stand in one position for so long that their joints stiffen and can no longer be used. Having completely lost the ability to walk, such a man rolls his body when he wants to move. Rolling their bodies, these ascetics cover incredibly long distances and visit many places of pilgrimage. Some ascetics are said to lie for a long time on a bed of nails.

Many ascetics cover parts of their body with ashes, since in Hinduism ashes represent primal matter. Ascetics can often be recognised by their possessions, for instance the staff often topped by a skull, phallus or a trident.

Most Indian holy men move constantly from one place to another, but some stay put for months, even years. An ascetic may lie naked in the grass so that after a year or so his body is covered almost completely with creepers.

Indian holy men are credited with supernatural powers. Some can suspend their breathing; some become totally oblivious of the effects of high or very low temperature; some lower their respiratory rate so that it is almost imperceptible; others remain without food or drink for weeks. It is also claimed that some holy men can make themselves invisible. Ascetics are even said to remain alive when buried in a grave; they can suspend their heart beat for some time and stay alive when a normal person would certainly die.

Holy men are said to be able to make themselves infinitely large or small.

Scientists explain that some of the powers which ascetics claim to possess may be the result of the influence of mind-altering drugs.

Some Indian holy men spend their whole lives in complete seclusion. They live in dense forests alone or in a cave in the mountains where they have no contact with the outside world. Such ascetics have a miserable life as they eat very little and often die of starvation. They are said to become real 'living skeletons' before they die.

Urine as a Key to Paradise

It seems absurd that some people used to drink human urine in order to get 'high'; nevertheless, in north-eastern Siberia there were people who used to do precisely that. Although urine by itself does not have any narcotic effects, if a person consumes certain plants the narcotic substances in that plant later pass intact into the urine. People must have been strongly addicted to this particular plant if they were ready to drink someone else's urine just to experience its mind-bending effect.

The plant with such incredible power is fly agaric, a common poisonous mushroom with a red cap spotted with white. Although this mushroom is found all over northern Europe and Asia and also in Australia it is rare in Siberia.

So in Siberia it was very expensive and only a few people could afford to buy it for pleasure. The urine of the people who had consumed it became a drink in Siberia. One eyewitness reported: 'Those who cannot afford to lay in a store of these mushrooms post themselves on these occasions around the huts of the rich and watch the opportunity of the guests coming down to make water and then hold a wooden bowl to receive the urine, which they drink greedily, as having still some virtue of the mushroom in it and by this they also get drunk'.

The mushrooms were collected in the tundra and then dried and made into pellets to be easily chewed and swallowed. Only fifteen minutes after eating them, the hallucinogenic effects of the mushroom commenced. They included unusual coloured visions as if of another world; this state of wellbeing could last for several hours.

Fly agaric was often used by local shamans who claimed that they were able to contact the spirit world in the deep narcotic trance caused by the mushrooms.

Fly agaric has the unusual power to alter human perception. Small wonder that since antiquity people have regarded this mushroom as sacred. Some 3500 years ago fly agaric was worshipped in some regions. When the Aryans came to settle in what is today northern India, they brought with them the cult of the fly agaric. This plant was their god Soma. Some country people even nowadays believe that by consuming the sacred mushroom they experience the miraculous presence of this god.

Note that consuming fly agaric even in a small dose is highly dangerous. The mushroom is so toxic that the 'wonderful trip' of those who take the risk and eat it for pleasure may be their last. Many cases of lethal poisoning by this mushroom have been reported all over the world.

Human Sacrifice in Europe

Human sacrifice has been practised in Europe. In the ancient city of Abdera in Thrace (Greece) human sacrifice was performed every year in the belief that the victim would carry away with him all the sins of the people. In Athens, human sacrifice was performed for a different reason. When a calamity struck, a special sacrifice was made which involved the death of two victims, a man and a woman. The female was sacrificed to protect all the women in the city while the man was offered to protect men. The chosen victims were brought to the gate of the city and stoned to death. It was believed that the two victims would carry away all the sins which had brought the calamity, a prolonged drought or an epidemic.

Sacrificial victims were normally chosen from among the so-called 'degraded and useless' persons who were kept at public expense to be used for sacrifice when needed. But in the Greek colony then in Marseilles, when an epidemic of plague erupted, there was always a volunteer who was ready to be used as a sacrificial victim. It was usually a very poor man because for a period of time he could lead the life of a rich man, as the community generously supported such a volunteer. For a whole year, sometimes, the poor man was treated like a hero. He was provided with the most attractive clothes and excellent food. On the fatal day the man, beautifully decorated with flowers and ceremonially dressed, was led in procession accompanied by a crowd. When the procession reached the gate of the city, the man went outside the city walls where he was stoned to death.

Another kind of human sacrifice was practised by the Greeks of the Near East until the end of the sixth century BC. It was customary to sacrifice the most ugly or deformed person. The man was led by the crowd to a special place where his body was uncovered and his genitals were ritually struck seven times with quills in an effort to eliminate the influence of the evil spirits. While the assembled people played flutes and sang, a great fire was prepared from tree branches. When it was burning strongly, the victim was thrown into the flames and burned alive. His ashes were later collected and thrown into the sea to carry away all the people's sins.

Bizarre Temple

People piously pray in a temple while snakes of all sizes slither around. Yet the people seem to pay no attention to them, and continue to pray as if the snakes were not there. This is an everyday scene in a Chinese temple in Penang, Malaysia. Every tourist can witness it daily, even now. And the snakes are said to be poisonous.

Visitors are assured that the snakes only rarely bite the worshippers. And the snakes are well fed and rather lazy, so they do not move much.

The famous temple is located on the way to Bayan Lepas Airport. Visitors can see snakes curling around tree branches placed on the altar. Coiling and entwining themselves in peculiar poses, the snakes seem to own the place.

The temple was built in the middle of the nineteenth century and thirty years later it was reconstructed and enlarged. People of Penang tell the following story to explain the origin of the snakes in the temple. Where the temple is situated, there was the house of a man who was famous for his healing power. When he died the people decided to commemorate his deeds by building a temple. But when the temple was erected snakes seemed to have chosen to live there and since then they have been regarded as disciples of the famous man.

The bizarre temple is considered by tourists, especially those from Europe and the USA, as a temple in which snakes are worshipped. This is not true, and thus many guide books are misleading. Some authors erroneously state that 'the snake is placed on a tray and worshipped' in the Penang temple. There is no snake worship in this temple although it may seem so as they are kept there and fed.

Untouchables

In India there were millions of people who by Hindu tradition were not allowed to touch other people because of the fear of pollution. These people were believed to have an inborn impurity which has a polluting effect on other people. These people, known as untouchables, are traditionally placed by Hindus outside the Indian caste system. Members of castes made every effort to avoid contact with them. Untouchables were treated in the past as if they were not human beings. As James Forbes noted in the early nineteenth century: 'If a Nair accidentally meets a Pooleah on the highway, he cuts him down with as little ceremony as we should destroy a noxious animal'. Untouchables were prohibited from using public roads or 'even to breathe the same air' as members of higher castes. If an untouchable saw at a distance a member of a high caste walking in his direction, he immediately had to make a loud warning by howling and then hide himself by climbing up the nearest tree.

In areas inhabited by high castes such as Brahmins, untouchables were not allowed out of their houses during day time. As late as 1932, according to an Indian newspaper report, certain groups of untouchables called Purada-Vannah were obliged to live a nocturnal existence and were classified as unseeable.

Even purchasing goods from a shop belonging to higher caste members was a problem for an untouchable. To avoid the 'dangerous' contact with the shopkeeper an untouchable had to behave in a special way. It was customary for him to place money in front of the shop and withdraw to a distant place. The shopkeeper would then take his money and place the purchased goods on the ground. After the shopkeeper was back in his shop, the untouchable collected his goods.

There were even restrictions on clothing of untouchables.

In some parts of India untouchables were forbidden to wear ordinary sandals, use umbrellas or wear dresses made of silk. The women were prohibited from wearing gold ornaments and were not even allowed to cover their breasts.

Despite the untouchables being outside the Indian caste system, they themselves are divided into hundreds of castes. Those who belong to higher castes within the untouchables would become polluted if they touched or made contact with those who are lower. If a member of the Nayadi caste comes near a member of Pooleah, who is a member of a higher untouchable caste he must perform a cleansing ceremony. He would take seven baths and in addition would scratch his little finger and shed blood to make purification effective.

There was a special scale of distances within which members of a given untouchable caste could approach a member of the Brahmin caste. Such a 'safe' distance was 29 metres for a Pariah but it was only seven metres for a 'less polluting' Kammalan.

When India gained independence in 1949, the traditional discrimination against the untouchables was legally abolished. Despite this the social status of untouchables remains depressed and in some rural areas of India the old customs are still observed. Even nowadays those who decide to employ untouchables in their houses as servants fear pollution and avoid direct contact with them. When they give them food or water, it is done in a special way. Water will be poured into a cup placed on the porch so that it would not be touched by the master. The untouchable servant then drinks from the cup and sets it back in place.

In some regions members of higher castes behave as if no changes to traditional discrimination have occurred. If the shadow of an untouchable falls upon food eaten by a caste member he would throw it away considering it to be polluted. Despite the existing law, in some villages untouchables are still prohibited from drawing water from the common village well.

Untouchables still perform the despised and dirty work of India. Their traditional occupations are collecting garbage, cleaning latrines and so on. Since a Hindu considers handling animal skins as polluting, caste members are not allowed to play drums covered with animal skin. Playing musical instruments including drums traditionally is the job open to untouchables.

Dangerous Holy Service

Indian snake charmers are famous for their frightening acts of enticing deadly cobras from their baskets but that is child's play compared with the snake-handlers of the USA. What is even more surprising is that snake handling does not take place there to impress visitors but is part of a solemn ritual, inside Christian churches.

Snakes used in these services are the most dangerous, and include rattlesnakes and copperheads. The snakes are kept in large boxes inside the church.

During the ceremony a special rope is stretched out around the dangerous box to separate visitors from the worshippers. While the preaching is going on and hymns are being sung, the snakes are kept closed in the box. But when the emotions of the devotees reach a proper level the snake box is opened and a believer snatches one of the deadly snakes from the box. After holding it in his hands for a while he offers it to another waiting devotee. In this way one snake after another is removed from the box and passed from one to another by the worshippers.

Great prestige is attached to the first and 'bravest' one who takes the first snake from the 'angry knot' in the box. That is the most dangerous moment.

Some worshippers handle the snakes in a rather peculiar way, pushing the snake under their shirt or kissing it. This procedure indicates a complete lack of fear. As Weston La Barre describes the snake-handling in one of the churches of this sect in Tennessee: 'A buxom elderly gap-toothed woman—who walked barefoot among seventeen buzzing rattlesnakes in a homecoming service in the summer of 1946—held a beautiful large timber rattler around her neck like a necklace with the free neck and head of the snake along the outside of her left forearm, while cooing with closed eyes and a delighted expression on her face'.

Some observers suspected that the snakes used in the worship of this sect had been deprived beforehand of their deadly fangs, but that is not true. Devotees of the cult are frequently bitten by the snakes, but they usually 'miraculously' recover.

However, when a devotee dies as a result of 'unfortunate' snake-handling, it is regarded as the will of the Lord. Such cases do not discourage others from the strange and dangerous practices. They admit that although they fear snake bites, the deadly snake-handling is the best demonstration of their faith in God.

The snake-handling cult was founded by G. Went Hensley in 1909. He introduced the practice in some churches in Tennessee and Kentucky. He pointed out that in the gospel of St Mark it is written that true believers in God 'shall pick up serpents'. So he concluded that snake-handling must be performed in 'obedience to Scripture'.

Some authors suggest that the snake-handling cult has arisen from the well-known ceremonies of some North American Indian tribes, who practised rites using deadly snakes.

The cult founder himself was bitten by a poisonous snake when he was 70 years old, and although it could have been a fatal bite, he soon recovered. His followers regarded this event as a miracle from God.

The dangerous cult has developed in several States of the USA but has been prohibited in some States. Followers, however, are ready to travel great distances to where the practice is allowed, or they simply perform the ritual in secret.

14.
Weird Festivals and Celebrations

Dance of Death

Some tantrics of Tibet used to perform the so-called Chod ceremony which was among the most incredible and disgusting religious rituals that ever existed. It was performed only at the dismembering ground where dead bodies were not actually buried but left to be devoured by scavenging animals. It was the place where according to Tibetan tradition the corpses of humans were brought and cut into pieces to facilitate the feast of the animals. The word chod actually means 'to dismember'.

As well as these tantrics choosing the most unpleasant place to carry out their rites, they decorated their bodies in the most horrific way. Before the rite they searched for the remains of the human corpses and decorated their bodies with aprons made of pieces of human skin and bones. Wearing such regalia they then performed a macabre dance of death. During the rite they were trying to imagine that their own bodies were cut into pieces like those of the corpses. So they acted as if they were suffering from immense pain caused by the operation. However, unlike the corpses, they conceived that they were dismembered while still being alive. They then imagined that their body was devoured by monstrous demons.

Practitioners of this horrific rite claimed that there was nothing wrong with their performance as it was designed to make them ritually dead and then spiritually reborn. They explained that this was just a variant of the initiation rite in which the tantrist rises symbolically from death. They said that their chod dance aimed at cutting away 'the false concept of ego by offering one's own body to demons'.

These odd practices were described by W. I. Evans-Wentz in 1935. He noted that 'the Chod rite has been practised in the recent past and probably is still practised although with great discretion'.

Human Pincushions

Cruel religious celebrations involving incredible self-mortification can be observed in various parts of the world, even in Singapore. The Indian community there celebrates annually a festival called Thaipusan in honour of Subramanian, a god with six heads and twelve arms who personifies youth, virtue and power. He is the eldest son of Siva. The festival takes place annually on 20 January and it includes a procession to the Chettiar Temple in Tank Road.

During the festival Hindus carry out vows of self-mortification made when they were seriously sick. In most cases this involves carrying 'kawadis' during the procession. As J. Wong explains: 'Kawadis are wooden or steel arches with bars for support on the shoulders. From the outside of each arch, copper spikes, usually about thirty in number, are fixed so that their points enter the carrier's body rather like the spokes of a bicycle wheel'. Each arch with its spokes weighs about 17 kilograms.

Many devotees carry smaller burdens of their own choice which are attached through small fish-hooks to their flesh. It is usually their breasts and backs which provide space for the burden. Some men carry a large number of small milk containers made of steel, others carry many oranges. Other devotees pierce their tongues or cheeks with silver needles or trident-like spikes of steel.

Women are only allowed to carry small burdens attached to their flesh superficially. Even small children may undergo some form of self-mortification for this god during the celebration.

Participants in the more severe forms of self-mortification must especially prepare themselves for the event. They are allowed only one meal a day and they must totally abstain from alcoholic drinks before the festival, and twenty-four hours before the event they must fast. They must also refrain from sexual intercourse and immoral thoughts, and since no contact with menstruating women is allowed, they have to sleep on the floor. They must also remain unshaven and they cannot use utensils previously touched by other people. Those men with a family member who has recently died are not allowed to mortify themselves during the event. The festival was once popular in India but was outlawed there because of the cruelty involved.

Similar self-tortures are employed by Chinese spirit mediums. According to a travel guide to Singapore, on the birthday of the Chinese monkey god, who is believed to have the power to cure every sickness 'assuming the personality of various gods, but mostly that of the Monkey God himself, they skewer their cheeks, tongues and arms, plunge their arms into boiling oil, scourge themselves with spike-balls, roll on knife-blades or climb a knife-ladder with upturned knife-blades as rungs'. Similar self-torture can be observed on the birthday of the Saint of the Poor.

Self-mortification ceremonies resembling those described above are also performed by some Muslims. The Qaderi dervishes of Kurdistan in Iran (a breakaway Islamic sect) are famous for their acts of self-mortification. As one eyewitness reported in 1973 'Young boys licked red-hot metal spoons and pushed skewers through their cheeks. Men ate glass and long nails and drove swords through the skin around their stomachs.'

During the Sri Lankan festival known as Kataragama, people from many faiths including Muslims, Christians, Hindus and Buddhists all come to worship God and many inflict self-mortification. Walter Gamage, a British ex-sailor, is among those who take part annually in this festival as he fulfils a vow to God given earlier. He puts 108 pins in his body. He explains: 'I feel that when I do these things I satisfy God, and I get his full protection. Being a human being I don't think I can live without his protection'.

Snake Dance

The Hopi Indians of Arizona (USA) used to worship the rattlesnake, one of the most deadly in the world. Hopi believed that these snakes had a miraculous power to bring rain. From this belief their peculiar cult of the rattlesnake evolved. During a prolonged drought and danger of famine, the Hopi organised a special festival to honour the snakes and beg them for rain.

Before the festival date the local priests ordered their men to collect as many rattlesnakes as possible. The men searched for several days, collecting snakes which were brought to the village. The snakes were washed and then placed inside the special bower located in the middle of the village.

With a snake in his mouth and without using his hands, the priest then began his peculiar dance. One by one the other priests took snakes from the bower and performed their dance. When the dance was over, each priest placed the snake back in the bower to rest. All the snakes were then taken back to the forest and released. After such a ceremony Hopi believed the rattlesnakes which were honoured by men would be willing to carry the message of the people to the appropriate gods who would bring the expected rain.

It is said that despite the casual treatment of the snakes during the ceremonial dance, the snakes have never bitten their worshippers. Some authors argue that the snakes behave because during the monotonous dance the snake is put into a state of catalepsy which makes them temporarily harmless.

Public Flagellation

One day in 1973 the authors themselves witnessed a strange procession in Baghdad in Iraq. The procession was headed by a group of half-naked men, walking slowly and flagellating themselves with iron chains with such force that blood was dripping from their wounded backs and staining their white robes. A group of very young boys also took part in this parade, beating their backs with similar but smaller chains. The boys were brought there by their parents who were grateful to God for delivering to them a son.

This unusual celebration resembling a funeral was performed by the Shia Muslims of Baghdad. The ceremony was to commemorate the martydom of Husain, the grandson of Mohammed. In the seventh century Husain was lured to Kerbala where he was attacked and slain by religious opponents. He was buried at Kerbala and the tragic death of the saint is re-enacted each year. It is performed on the tenth day of the lunar month of Muharram.

This sad ceremony of public flagellation was later abolished in Iraq.

Similar celebrations were also known in Turkey, involving an even gorier show. As one eyewitness of a public flagellation in Istanbul in the early twentieth century reported 'A ghostly-looking crew of men, clad in long white robes, with uncovered heads and naked swords in their hands. These men numbered many hundreds . . . flourished their naked swords, slashed them widely, and occasionally turned the points on themselves or their companions, gashing heads, faces, and breasts until the blood flowed and discoloured their white robes'. This group of swordsmen was accompanied by a large group of fanatics who performed self-flagellation using chains.

Flagellation was also known among the early Christians. They considered the self-inflicted whipping the best method of repressing fleshly urges. As human flesh was believed to be the source of all sins, flagellation was demanded by religious ascetics. One of the cardinals of the Christian church in eleventh century Europe was enthusiastic about this drastic method used to scourge evils; he noted that '1000 self-inflicted lashes are the spiritual equivalent of ten penitential psalms'.

Religious flagellation was so popular in thirteenth and fourteenth century Europe that special groups were formed called the Brotherhood of Flagellants. They considered self-inflicted whippings the best way of praising God. Although these groups were officially condemned by church authorities, flagellation was performed in convents and in public. As one author notes, in fourteenth century Germany, flagellation was a typical public activity: 'The flagellants massed in public, vast crowds of partly naked men and women, lashing themselves and each other twice daily for 33½ days, with devices ranging from little cords to leather thongs knotted and holding metal points, for the more extensive spilling of blood'.

Incredible Car Festival

One of the most fantastic festivals takes place in the town of Puri in Orissa state in India. It is celebrated in June to commemorate the journey of the God Vishnu from Gokul to Mathura. In this celebration it is not Vishnu but his incarnation Lord Jagannath who is worshipped. His wooden image and those of his brother and sister are normally kept inside the famous Jagannath Temple. Only once a year are these images taken from the temple and drawn in special procession through the street to another temple known as 'Garden House'.

The interesting part of this journey of gods is the form of transport. The great images are placed on especially constructed wooden cars called raths. These cars are incredibly large. The largest is 14 m high and 10 m square. Each car runs on sixteen wheels, each of which is more than 2 m in diameter. To put such colossal cars in motion necessitates the force of some 4000 car-pullers. The English word 'juggernaut' meaning 'slow and irresistible destructive force' comes from the word Jagannath.

Because of the tremendous force of thousands of car-pullers it is virtually impossible to stop the moving vehicles if an accident happens. As late as the nineteenth century, during this festival some devotees deliberately plunged themselves beneath the wheels of the chariot committing public self-sacrifice. The explanation for such a bizarre act was that some of the devotees wished to die in the god's sight.

When the colossal cars reach the Garden House it is the end of their ceremonial journey. The images of the gods are removed from the cars and placed in the temple. It is said that the gods must rest for seven days. After the gods have rested, the ceremonial journey is repeated with the same splendour, this time back to the Jagannath Temple.

After the return journey, the wooden cars are broken up and the pieces are used as holy relics. New cars are constructed for the celebration in the coming year.

Saturnalia

There was a curious festival in the Roman Empire during which slaves occupied all state positions and even had the power to make laws. In other words slaves became consuls, praetorians and senators. Furthermore, masters were supposed to serve their slaves who ate first. Only when they had finished were their masters allowed to dine.

Roles changed to such an extent that in every household slaves were in charge and made all the decisions. Slaves could even insult their masters, who were not allowed to punish them in any way. During the festival a special emperor was chosen whose behaviour was both comic and stupid. When, for example, he was making a speech, he was supposed to make fun of himself.

This weird festival was known as Saturnalia. It was organised in honour of the god Saturn, who was the patron of sowing and agriculture. He was said to have been the king of Rome long ago.

The Romans believed that during his reign there were abundant harvests and that it was a period of great happiness uninterrupted by disagreements or wars. At that time there was said to be no private property and no desire to gain profit. There was also no slavery. When the festival of Saturn was celebrated there was an attempt to recreate for a short time the conditions which were said to have existed during Saturn's reign. During the festival everybody was supposed to be happy and to have fun.

Unfortunately, even this joyful celebration was tragic for some. In parts of the Roman Empire it was customary to make human sacrifice at the end of the festival. Whoever was chosen to impersonate Saturn was obliged to commit suicide by cutting his throat at the altar. During the festival the chosen man could enjoy every pleasure, even the most immoral.

In one case in AD 303 a Roman soldier named Dasius was chosen to impersonate Saturn. Being a devoted Christian, he refused to become a mock pagan god. Because of this act of insubordination, the brave soldier was immediately slain. He was a Christian martyr and was later declared a saint of the Roman Catholic Church.

Feast of Fools

An unusual festival, known as the Feast of Fools, was celebrated during the Middle Ages in Europe, especially in France and Italy. It was a burlesque religious festival in which the sacred Christian mass was transformed into a peculiar and foolish farce. It was organised not by the enemies of the church but by the pious clergy themselves. The festival was usually held in mid-December and lasted several days.

At the beginning of the festival the positions of bishop and archbishop were given to the lowest clergy stratum, ignoring normal church law. These men were provided with the robes appropriate to the positions and they behaved as if they really were eminent church dignitaries. Holding their pastoral staffs, they were entitled to give solemn benedictions and blessing to the people.

The mass celebrated by them in the town cathedral however, had nothing to do with a normal celebration. It was a mock mass during which the mock bishop was assisted by mock clergy dressed in women's clothing. Instead of normal solemn prayers, obscene songs were sung and jovial dances were performed at the altar.

During this incredible service, clergy behaved as if they were not in a temple but in an ordinary restaurant, since they were eating sausages and playing cards at the altar. Instead of the usual incense they used to burn old shoes.

Although efforts were made to abolish this custom it was so popular among the clergy and people that it survived in Europe till the Reformation. As late as 1645 the Feast of Fools was celebrated in some monasteries in France. One author described this strange event in the following words: 'They hold in their hands books turned upside down, and pretend to read them through spectacles in which for glass have been substituted bits of strange peel . . . they do not sing hymns or psalms, or masses, as is customary; they mutter confused words, and utter cries as foolish, disagreeable, and discordant as those of a troop of grunting swine'.

He condemned these excesses by saying: 'For it would be better to bring brute beasts into church, to praise God in their own manner than to suffer this sort of folk to appear therein, who make a mock of God while pretending to praise him, and are more foolish and senseless than the most foolish and senseless beasts'.

A strange variation of this famous festival was held in the cathedral of Sens (France) where it was called the Feast of Ass. In this case an ass was led in procession by the clergy to the church. During the mock mass held there, the ass was the centre of burlesque ceremonies which lasted hours.

Boy Bishop

One of the queerest customs of medieval England was that of electing a boy bishop. The election to this strange position was performed during a special happy festival organised in honour of St Nicholas, the patron of children. Each year on 5 December, the young boys who belonged to the choir of the church or served at the altar during mass, elected a young bishop from among themselves. He was called boy bishop. They were commonly referred to as 'Nicholas and his clerks'.

Although this juvenile dignitary retained his post for only about three weeks, he exercised nearly all the powers of a real bishop. The boy bishop, equipped with his pastoral crozier, was invited by nobles to their houses as it was a great privilege to entertain such an eminent personality.

Even ruling monarchs respected the boy bishop. For example, King Edward I in 1299 invited a boy bishop with his clergy to the royal chapel at Hetton, near Newcastle-upon-Tyne. The boy bishop was asked to conduct their evening service.

Wearing ceremonial robes, both the boy bishop and his 'clergy' were later busy in the streets collecting donations for the church.

During the temporary episcopacy, a boy bishop and his clergy played their role very seriously. They recited prayers, and during the procession inside the church the real dignitaries had to serve him and his juvenile clergy by carrying candles. As one author noted: 'Wearing his mitre, and holding his pastoral staff in his left hand, the boy bishop gave a solemn benediction to all present'. The most difficult task for the boy bishop in his religious function appears to have been preaching a sermon during the mass. But there was in fact no problem at all. The adult bishop used to provide a boy bishop with a written sermon especially prepared for such an occasion. The full text of one of such sermons spoken by one of the boy bishops is still preserved in a museum.

It is hard to believe but the custom was so seriously treated by the community that if it happened that a boy bishop died during the festival, he was not buried as an ordinary person but with all the honours accorded to a real bishop.

While most people, especially the young, considered this custom as most amusing, such mock church ceremonies were not acceptable to some. Church reformers were against the practice and considered them defaming. One such was Cranmer, who in 1542 wrote a special appeal to the ruling king asking him to eradicate this 'dangerous superstition'.

The peculiar custom evolved in thirteenth century England and survived for centuries. With the establishment of Protestantism in England it was abolished.

15.
Cannibals and Head Hunters

A Net Full of Skulls

Among the head-hunting tribes of the world the most enthusiastic were no doubt the Dayaks of Borneo. To a Dayak male, life without a human head trophy was unthinkable. Possession of at least one such macabre trophy was an absolute necessity for a man who wanted to have a wife. To marry a girl from Dayak aristocracy even one human head was insufficient. One visitor heard from a Dayak: 'No aristocratic youth dares venture to pay his address to a Dayak demoiselle unless he throws at the blushing maiden's feet a net full of skulls'.

An amusing story is told about an eighteen-year-old boy who could not marry his girl because he was unable to bring her a precious head trophy. This happened in 1880, at the time when it was almost impossible to slay a man from a neighbouring tribe. To remedy the situation, with the help of his friend, the boy decided to decapitate a Chinese trader living nearby. He reasoned that by thoroughly boiling this head nobody would recognise its origin. Pretending to be travellers the boys went to the trader's house and asked him for lodging. In the middle of the night they attacked the merchant who, unexpectedly, was not sleeping so he cried loudly for help. Some fifty men ran to his rescue but the boys escaped, though without the 'trophy'.

Human heads were required for many other occasions. When a child was born to a chief of a village, the baby could not be named unless a freshly slain head was provided for the event by the father. Furthermore, the death of a chief meant that a human head was necessary so that the soul of the dead man would serve the chief in the afterlife. And an unpleasant prophecy in a chief's dream could be prevented from fulfilment by taking a human head. The head-hunting of Dayaks was linked to their religion. They believed that every major event upset the so-called cosmic balance in dangerous ways, and in order to restore that balance sacrifice of a human head was necessary.

Surprisingly, Dayak head hunters believed that severed human heads continue to live. Among the Sea Dayaks, after the head of a slain person was brought to shore it was wrapped in palm leaves. It was kept for months as an object of deep reverence and flattering speech. Tasty food was placed in the mouth, and even cigars were put between its lips. Occasionally, such heads were treated as adopted sons of the tribe.

To collect as many human heads as possible, the Dayaks organised large-scale expeditions. They usually studied in advance the customs of neighbouring tribes so that they could attack them when least expected. They often attacked a village just before daybreak, when the people were asleep. By throwing 'fire-balls' on the huts, they caused them to burst into flames and the people who tried to escape were mercilessly hacked to pieces. The flame gave sufficient light to distinguish between men and women and this was important as men were usually slain on the spot.

Their heads were then triumphantly carried back to the village while those who were captured alive were kept as slaves and were only slain when their heads were needed. When a head was cut off, the brain was extracted and the 'empty' head was held over a fire for a period of time to preserve it. Head trophies were carried in special baskets. Some warriors were able to collect hundreds. One Dayak chief named Selgie was said to have obtained seven hundred heads during a single expedition.

Incredible Lust for Human Flesh

The cruellest cannibals in the world were no doubt the Fijians. The victims themselves had to prepare everything necessary for their own roasting. They had to dig a hole in the earth to make the oven, cut firewood and make a cup from a banana-leaf. When everything was ready, the cannibals opened the victim's vein, filled the banana-leaf cup with his blood and drank it in the presence of the suffering man. Next, the cannibals cut off the arms and legs of their victim while he was still alive.

These parts of his body were then cooked in the oven and eaten in the presence of the still living victim. Sometimes the victim was even forced to eat parts of his own body before his death. The next step of this grisly feast involved eating the tongue which was pulled out of the victim with a fish-hook. The tongue was pulled out as far as possible and then cut off to be roasted and eaten while the unbearably suffering victim watched.

These macabre feasts involved eating more than one or two human beings. As a missionary wrote in 1836: 'The attendants bring into the circle baked human beings—not one, nor two, nor ten, but twenty, thirty, forty, fifty in a single feast. We have heard on credible authority of 200 human beings having been devoured on one of these occasions'.

This was no exaggeration. The habit of eating humans was such a common custom that no important business in Fiji could be initiated without offering a fresh victim. Even construction of a new canoe required a human sacrifice to ensure success. As Alfred St Johnson noted at the end of the nineteenth century: 'When a canoe had to be built, first a man had to be slain for laying of the keel . . . More men were used at its launching as rollers to aid its passage to the sea . . . after the canoe was afloat still more victims were required at the first taking down of the mast'.

The Fijians' lust for human flesh was so strong that it was common to kill and eat even a friend to satisfy the urge. Rev. John Watsford noted in 1846: 'A chief at Rakeraki . . . if he saw anyone, even one of his friends, was fatter than the rest, he had him or her killed at once and part roasted and part preserved'.

The lust for human flesh and the almost absolute rule of a husband over his wife in the old days, meant that it was quite lawful for a husband to kill and then eat his own wife.

The habit of eating human flesh was so popular among Fijians that human meat was even eaten by small children: 'The tribesmen chew little bits of raw human flesh as sailors chew tobacco and then put them in their children's mouth'.

Horrific Ritual

Among the Kwakiutl Indians of the north-west coast of Canada there was a strange sect of cannibals called the Hamatsas. They had a supreme god who was portrayed as a bear-like monster with gaping blood-stained mouth; he had the unusually long name,

Baxbakualanuxsiwae, meaning 'he who is first to eat men at the mouth of the river'. Anyone who wanted to become a member of this sect had to pass a most bizarre initiation ritual.

First, the candidate had to live in seclusion in the forest for some three months in order 'to absorb the spirits' of the cannibals' supreme god. When the elders came out to meet the novice, his duty was to prepare a ceremonial meal for the ritual cannibal feast. But among the Hamatsas such a meal had to be flesh from the body of a dead person. It was not difficult to find such a 'meal' because it was customary among the Kwakiutls to inter their dead in trees.

The body of the dead person was first soaked in salt water and then smoked over a fire, before being put in the tree.

At the initiation feast, each Hamatsa, in strict order of seniority, had to pick up a portion of the corpse. During the feast, the flesh had to be swallowed whole and then vomited up. This was helped by a drink of salt water, which resulted in a violent fit of vomiting. The ceremony of 'eating' human flesh was carefully observed by the others to make sure that the number of gobbets swallowed agreed with those vomited out. The aim of this horrific meal was to show the novice that, like the elder sect members, he had lost all his normal human qualities and become a true disciple of the supreme god of cannibals.

After the feast, the novice had to return to his village, sit on the roof of his hut, and wait for passersby. Personifying a ferocious beast he then had to jump down and bite some flesh from them.

The rite culminated when he descended from the roof and began to dance in convulsive fits. The dance ended with the arrival of a witch doctor, who dragged the exhausted man to the sea to calm him down.

Becoming a true sect member, the man would now regularly participate in battles, with the aim of obtaining fresh human flesh for cannibal feasts.

The Hamatsas' lust for human flesh was so strong that there were cases of members snatching a mouthful of flesh from the arms or breasts of their own sect members. According to one report, a Hamatsa man once asked his slave girl to dance for him. The terrified girl said 'I will dance. But do not get hungry. Do not eat me'. Hardly had she finished speaking, the story says, than her master split her skull with an axe and began eating her flesh.

Head Shrinkers

In the midst of the Amazon jungle in Ecuador lives one of the most ferocious tribes of South America, the Jivaros, notorious head hunters. They engage in head hunting and they actually shrink the decapitated human heads. This is not just minor head shrinking. They have perfected their art to such an extent that a large human head is reduced to little bigger than a human fist. What is even more remarkable is that the face's character remains unaltered. In fact such a shrunken human head becomes a perfect replica of the original head.

To accomplish it, all the flesh and bones are removed. The skin of the head is cooked in a special herbal concoction for about two hours, until it becomes rubbery. It is then sewn up and put on a pole to dry in the sun. Afterwards, hot pebbles are inserted inside the 'head' and rolled around. As a result of this treatment the size of the original head is reduced almost by half. When the head is too small to 'take' the pebbles, hot sand is placed inside, causing the head to shrink even more. Finally, it acquires the desired size. The hair, which is still its original length, contributes to the shrunken head's macabre appearance. It is further decorated with birds' feathers, augmenting the terrifying effect.

To prevent the escape of the dead man's vengeful soul, which is believed to inhabit the shrunken head, the lips and eyelids are sewn up and the nostrils are plugged with cotton. In fact, the whole act of head shrinking was invented in the strong belief that if the head was not treated this way, the dead soul would escape through its openings and turn itself into a vengeful demon, killing the warrior who had slain it.

Despite these precautions the dead man's soul is still believed to be able to inflict harm. To prevent it, special rites are performed after the head has been shrunk.

During the night after the man was killed there is a feast at which warriors drink hallucinogenic potions. These change their minds and they remain for a long time in a state of ecstasy. Then the warrior who took the head stays in seclusion for three days to be purified. The shrunken head lies on a shield beside the hut.

A witch doctor pours tobacco juice into the nostrils of the warrior to protect him against the action of evil spirits. The purification ceremony concludes when the witch doctor orders the warrior to ritually touch the hair of the shrunken head while reciting certain formulas.

Since so much effort is required to eliminate the danger from a slain head, why are the Jivaros such enthusiastic man killers? The Jivaros believe that in order to live for a long time a man needs to acquire the so-called aratum soul. If a man has an aratum soul he can only be killed by disease. Such a soul can only be obtained by experiencing a vision in the jungle, which is usually possible only by taking hallucinogenic drugs. Under the influence of drugs a man has a strong urge to kill, but when he kills a person he loses his aratum soul.

To the Jivaros the real world is the world of illusions and hallucinations. Thus, reality to a Jivaro is the world experienced under the influence of hallucinogenic plants. To perceive this world is so important to the Jivaros that an infant as young as just a few days old is given a hallucinogenic potion in order to introduce it to the 'real' world. The Jivaros do not believe, however, that it is sufficient just to introduce human beings to their world. Hunting dogs, which are their close companions, are also offered hallucinogenic potions for the same reason.

Cruel Inventors

The clerics who first came to northern Brazil soon learned about the existence of the ferocious Tupinamba peoples. These most dangerous cannibals were a great risk to the whites who came to bring Christianity to the region. In fact, in 1556, the first Bishop of Brazil together with some 100 whites was overpowered by the Tupinambas when his ship was wrecked. The natives stripped them all, slew them and devoured them.

Some whites miraculously escaped their fate and were able to describe the customs of the Tupinamba in detail. Among those who were lucky was Hans Staden, a German sailor. Although he was caught by Tupinambas near Santos in 1552, he survived by using a clever trick to fool his oppressors. When he saw that he was about to be killed and eaten, he refused to eat by feigning a horrible toothache. Later, he was too thin to be eaten. The Tupinambas decided to postpone the execution of their prisoner until he was fatter.

Then, to further postpone his death, he started to behave like a man with miraculous powers. He made several prophecies to the tribe and as some came true, he was declared by the Tupinambas to be an oracle of the whole tribe. Consequently he became too precious to be killed and eaten.

He lived for a long time among these cruel cannibals and he had a chance to get acquainted with all their strange customs. He learned with surprise that these primitive people used a 'poison gas' when attacking their enemies. The Tupinambas seem to have discovered 'poison gas' as a weapon much earlier than more advanced European nations.

Their military strategy was as follows. Close to the village to be attacked they first erected a huge pile of wood and lit a fire. When wind started blowing in the direction of the enemy huts, they added leaves and fruits of a certain noxious pepper plant. As a result an unbearably acrid smoke was produced which, like a poison gas, travelled with the wind and suffocated the people in their huts. This gas was so strong that it drove the besieged enemy away from the fortifications. As a result the defenders became temporarily vulnerable to attack by clever Tupinambas.

The cannibalistic practices of the Tupinambas arose from their strong belief in taking revenge for members of the tribe killed by their enemies. They believed that the only way to please their ancestors was to kill their enemies and eat them. The custom was so popular that any wrongdoing demanded the act of revenge. It was performed by simply biting off some of the flesh of the offender and consuming it on the spot. They were so obsessed with the necessity of revenge that they were said to often bite a stone if it hurt them when a person tripped upon it.

The Last Cannibals

The Dani of Irian Jaya practised cannibalism as late as the 1960s. They are said to be the last cannibals in the world. They were also the last discovered cannibals of the world, since the tribe remained unknown till 1938. As a former cannibal explained to a journalist in 1992: 'the main impetus was to absorb the spirit from a strong enemy. It would often be the person they most admired'. Although he is now a Christian the tribesman describes the old days with a sense of nostalgia: 'Old ones are tough . . . Young men and women taste better. And babies taste like fish. The flesh is very soft'.

The Dani practised the following customs associated with cannibalism. The man to be eaten was procured during battle with an enemy village. His body was tied to a pole and carried by four strong warriors. While the warriors were carrying their trophy, people from the defeated side watched from a distance and shouted angrily, demanding the corpse be returned for a decent burial. The victors, greatly excited and delighted, responded with the customary phrase: 'We are going to eat him'.

Hundreds of Dani warriors and their families, including small children, gathered outside the huts, eagerly waiting for the great feast to begin. When the corpse was placed on the ground it was immediately surrounded by dancing women, who shouted insults, jabbing the body with their sticks and stamping on it with their feet. While the women were dancing, the men were busy preparing a huge fire. Before the body was cooked, all its toes were cut off and then the rest of the body was cut into small pieces. When the body was cooked a great feast commenced. Two missionaries who witnessed the beginning of the ceremony were so terrified and disgusted that they ran away. They vowed they would never again attend such an horrific rite. They also tried unsuccessfully to expel from their minds the horrific things they had witnessed.

Power of the Left Eye

In the past, cannibalism was common among the Maoris, the indigenous people of New Zealand. Captain Cook and his men were the first Europeans to witness the Maoris' gruesome cannibal feasts. Captain Cook reported seeing the people gnawing human bones with 'an abolute lust, their hands and faces . . . smeared with blood while they picked fragments of human gristle from between their sharply filed teeth'. He also said that when they made an inquiry about some bones found on the beach they were told that 'about five days before, a boat belonging to their enemies came into the bay, with many persons on board, and that this man was one of the *seven* whom they had killed'.

No wonder early missionaries in this region had a great fear of being eaten by those whom they wanted to convert. Fortunately one of the Maori chiefs told them that they should not worry as their meat was not as delicious as that of the local people.

Surprisingly, although human brain was considered to be of a particular value it was the left eye of the slain enemy which was the most important. It was said to contain the soul of that person.

Although the left eye was important, it was the heart of the victim which was believed to have a miraculous power. Human heart was used as a sacrifice to the gods when the fate of the tribe was at great risk. This sacrifice was the more effective the more valuable was the chosen victim. A Maori chief once even offered the heart of his beloved son in order to magically defeat his enemies in a battle, and to defend his fort. When his son was brought to him he personally cut open his breast and offered the heart to the gods. In another incident the chief of the defending fort was sacrificed by his own people in order to bring victory over their enemies.

As a writer noted in 1904: 'When the Kaiapoi stronghold was attacked by forces of Raupaha, the heart of the chief of the defending party was cut out and roasted in the fire . . . The priest chanted and the warriors stretched out their arms towards the heart while it was cooking . . . the chief priest tore off a portion of the heart and threw it among the enemy to weaken them'.

Sometimes human heart was ritually eaten during the mourning ceremony after the death of their chief. The ritual of a heart was also used for rather trivial purposes. For example, when a tree for a chief's canoe was cut down, a human heart had to be provided to commemorate the event. Heart was even eaten at the tattooing of the lips of the chief's daughter.

When during battle the Maoris were able to seize an enemy chief they treated him in an extremely vengeful way. The man was slain, cooked and eaten, but all his bones were carefully gathered after the feast and used to demonstrate the greatest possible indignity to the dead chief. His bones were used to make fish-hooks, knives, or sharpened and used as points for their arrows or as barbs for catching birds.

Occasionally they used whole hands of the dead chief. His hands were dried, with his fingers bent towards the palm. Then the dried hands were fastened to the walls of houses to serve as hooks for hanging baskets.

All these customs were practised in order to show that even a dead enemy chief would remain forever the slave of those who conquered him.

16.
Death Rituals

Removal of Sexual Power

A very unusual burial custom has evolved among the Falis, who live in northern Cameroon in West Africa, particularly when a male family member dies. The corpse of a man is not buried immediately, but watched carefully by his relatives inside his hut for several days, until the body starts to decompose. Only then do they admit that their man has really died.

Before the burial the corpse is sat in an upright position in a chair with its hands stretched out in front. The whole corpse, except hands and feet, is tightly wrapped with cotton bands. The sexual organ of the deceased is treated in a special way; to demonstrate the virility of the dead man his penis is tied in an erect position.

To commemorate his death, the assembled people dance for several hours around the corpse to the rhythm of sacred drums. Then the corpse is wrapped in hides and the priest ritually kills two goats.

When this rite is over a man in a mask arrives and turns the corpse around seven times. The body is then carried to a sacred cemetery cave in a mountain.

Before the wrapped body is disposed in the cave, another important ritual must be performed. The priest pretends first to give the dead man his final meal and then mourners search for a fine stone. When the stone is brought, the priest hits the stone with a stick. By doing so he invites the spirit of the dead man to enter the stone and inhabit it for ever. The stone with the spirit in it is then placed by the priest between the legs of the dead man. This final rite aims at removing the sexual power of the deceased. The stone is now considered sacred and is placed in the cave with the many other sacred stones representing the spirits of ancestors who have passed away earlier.

Chocolate Coffins

Many peculiar customs are observed in honour of the dead. In Mexico, graveside picnics are organised on 2 November, All Souls Day. It is known in Mexico as the Day of the Dead and it is believed that on that day the dead come alive. To honour dead relatives, alcohol and food are offered by their families. In the case of dead children, toys are often offered.

Food offered is always in the shape of objects associated with death: chocolates in the shape of coffins and hearses, skulls made of sugar, funeral wreaths and skeletons and bread decorated with skull and crossbones. The food is afterwards eaten by the families of the deceased.

On that day many cars and taxis are decorated with small gold skeletons. In addition, in many parts of Mexico people erect altars to commemorate their deceased relatives. They put on them their favourite foods, brandy and even cigarettes.

Among the Mayas in the village of Chan Kom strange celebrations take place. Bones of people who were buried three years before, are removed from the graves. While the grave is open, a little holy water is sprinkled into the grave and the bones are blessed. After the bones have been removed, they are placed on a new piece of cloth, then cleansed and finally put into a box on another cloth, where they are again sprinkled with holy water. Afterwards the box is closed and carried to a shelter in the cemetery where the Lord's prayer is said over it. The box is then taken to the dead person's former home where it is put under a table of offerings. The priest says more prayers and then a table of food is offered to the bones and more food to the people present. At night more prayers are said and the box is again sprinkled with holy water. Eventually the box is taken back to the cemetery and left in the shelter.

Belief in the return of the dead on a particular day is not confined to Mexico. In Europe some peoples put plates of food on the tombs of their relatives on All Souls Day. In Naples in Italy a very bizarre custom used to be practised. Charnel-houses were opened, and the skeletons dressed up in robes and arranged in niches along the walls.

Passport for the Dead

Some Chinese believe that it is necessary from time to time to check how the spirits of dead members of the family are coping in the underworld, and whether they need anything. To find out, the services of a medium are used. Sometimes a spirit may be wandering aimlessly because it has forgotten its identity. If this happens, the medium will arrange a passport and visa to the underworld. The medium is usually an elderly woman. She contacts spirits of the dead in a trance.

The passport is a document about as big as a medium-sized poster. To prepare this the medium requires not only the name and date of birth of the dead person, but, if possible, the precise birth time to the minute.

The document has a red chop or seal, which is like a visa giving permission for entry to the underworld. After all this has been written, the document is placed by the medium before the altar in the corner of the room. Many other pieces of paper on which are written spells and charms against illness, danger and bad luck and various prayer incantations are added to the document. There is also provided a set of paper clothes for the dead person, and so-called hell bank notes.

Funeral without a Body

The Dogon of West Africa have a custom of performing a funeral ceremony without a body. The peculiar funeral takes place when a man has left home and has not been seen for a long time. For this, he is regarded as dead by his family.

The most surprising thing about this custom is that even if the man is later found to be alive, he is treated by everybody as dead. Even if he has been unable to contact his community for reasons beyond his control, no exception is made, and he is regarded as dead. Often, a message sent home by a man was lost on the way; the man is not guilty of negligence but nothing can be done to reverse the results of the funeral.

If the man returns safely home, even his spouse or children pretend not to know him.

His situation is really desperate. As a 'dead' person he has no right to own any property. He has lost everything he owned because after the funeral the wealth of the 'dead person' was distributed to his family. No matter how high his position in the community, his role has been transferred to another.

His family ignore the living person but make offerings to him at his ancestral shrine and his spirit continues to be venerated. He becomes the loneliest person in the community. His only means of survival is begging.

In some other societies a person who has violated the rules of his community is excluded by a form of funeral ceremony without a body. The mock funeral is a way of sending the message that the group considers him socially dead.

A variation of this practice is found among the Benedictine monks; when an initiate joins the order he must perform a kind of rite to show that he 'dies to the world' after taking his vow. The ritual closely resembles a funeral service.

Among some strict orthodox Jews there is the custom of wearing mourning clothes if a son or daughter marries a person of another faith.

Burial of a Living Person

An unusual burial custom used to be practised by the Dinka, the pastoral people of southern Sudan. They buried some of their people when they were still alive. It was not a cruel revenge on a hated enemy, but they did it to their most beloved and respected chiefs. The chiefs themselves requested the burial. It did not necessarily take place when the chief was seriously ill and about to die. Sometimes, the chief was still reasonably healthy.

According to one account, when a chief known as Deng Deng felt that his sight had become poor and his teeth had gone, he decided that the time had come for him to be buried alive in line with tribal custom. He informed his children that it was his wish to be buried alive and asked them to tell all the people about his decision, in order to get their permission for his burial.

The chief's wish was fulfilled; a very big grave was dug on the highest point of the cattle-camp site and the chief was placed on a shield made from the hide of a bull and lowered into the grave. His relatives and friends watched the ceremony and sang hymns. They began throwing cattle dung into the grave but they only partly covered the grave.

The voice of the chief could still be heard, and he made a final speech recalling the success of the tribe under his leadership and advising his people on how to act in the future. The people asked him questions and received answers literally from the grave.

So long as the conversation continued they did not cover the whole grave. But when the chief stopped replying, they covered the whole grave with dung. They then announced that the master 'has been taken into the earth', and a shrine was constructed over the grave.

Although there were certain variations in the rite among the Dinka, the burial was always inspired by the chief himself. His request to be buried alive had to be granted by the people so that the act was always the result of a collective decision. A chief was never buried against his will.

This unusual custom is based on the belief that if a chief who represents the spiritual welfare of the whole community dies as an ordinary man, a calamity will strike the tribe.

The macabre custom was officially banned by the British colonial authorities but was said to have survived till the end of the nineteenth century. Old customs however seem to fade slowly. When one of the famous Dinka chiefs died in a Cairo hospital in 1969, and his body was sent back to his home town for burial, people were disappointed. It was unfortunate, they said that the chief was already dead and could not be buried alive in accordance with custom.

Lord Cat

The Toraja people of Indonesia strongly believe that an everlasting paradise after death can only be achieved if an elaborate funeral ceremony takes place. It is a spectacular and joyful event and costs more than a wedding ceremony.

In the past, the death of a Toraja nobleman was first announced to his domestic cat. Usually, one of the relatives said: 'Dear Lord Cat, your master has died'. The cat had important status in the house as it was regarded as the guardian of all household possessions.

The funeral ceremony involves lengthy preparations, so the body is kept in a special ritual home and the death is not announced to the community for several months or even years. During this time the people do not refer to the deceased as dead but always as the 'sleeping one'.

The custom was that the soul of the dead man had to be accompanied by the soul of a buffalo. The number ritually slaughtered depended on the status of the deceased. For a respected community member at least twelve buffalo had to be offered, but there were cases when up to a hundred animals were killed. As one author noted: 'In fact the greater the number of buffalo sacrificed, the greater honour was given to the family of the deceased. For each ten animals slaughtered, the family was entitled to mount one buffalo horn outside their house, as a sign of dignity'.

A hundred years ago even human sacrifice was demanded during the funeral of a noble man.

The custom of buffalo sacrifice has been abandoned. Instead, buffalo fights and cockfighting take place and people bet on them. During a funeral in which thousands may participate, people seem to forget about the dead person and they appear to be full of joy. As one eyewitness said: 'I can't imagine a happier way of being seen off on the eternal journey'.

Such a funeral may last seven days, during which various rites are performed. At one moment the coffin is carried out from the house and laid on a bier, while the crowd chants and offers foods and various gifts in order to help the soul on the trip to heaven. The coffin is then carried around the estate of a wealthy Toraja man. During this last trip the coffin is frequently tossed in the air. This is not for fun. Shaking the body is carried out in the belief that movement will encourage the soul to leave the body. The celebration is over when the coffin is finally deposited in a deep burial cave and the entrance closed off.

Unlike in other regions, funeral chambers are located high up in the cliffs. The Toraja believe that from such a high elevation the spirit of the dead can more easily climb the nearest palm tree and ascend to heaven. The bodies of buried people are not left unguarded. The Toraja make almost an life-size wooden effigy of the dead person before burial. These dolls are housed on a cliff-side veranda. They have eyes made of seashells, and from a distance they look like living people contemplating the land below. The dolls stand in rows of up to ten effigies, as if they are presiding over the Toraja mortals left behind in the village.

Every year the village men climb the high vertical cliff of the cemetery to fetch the effigies of their dead to their former homes. The dolls are washed, dressed in new clothes and then returned to the cliff-side.

Mourners' Taboo

Among the Maori of New Zealand there was a harsh taboo to be observed by those who had any direct contact with the dead. The taboo had to be observed by anyone who touched a corpse, helped to carry a corpse to the grave or touched the bones of a dead person. The taboo was very harsh. A person was deprived for a specified time of contact with any other person. He or she had to completely cut links with the community. It was believed that if such a polluted person touched a living person he would transfer all evil. For this reason a person who took direct part in a funeral was not allowed to enter a house inhabited by other community members.

The taboo even extended to foods. It was believed that such an 'unclean' person should not touch food with his or her hands. Infected with evil, the hands were believed to be dangerous. It was customary to place food on the ground and the person had to eat it like an animal without using hands. Sometimes a person would be fed by another, who offered food with outstretched arms. But those who decided to feed such a person were themselves subjected to many unpleasant taboos.

Since everybody was afraid of having contact with those who had had contact with a corpse, in almost every village there was a special servant who took advantage of the custom. This person became a professional feeder. This was usually a very poor beggar, dressed in rags and with his body painted with red ochre. He usually sat in silence apart from others. He himself was fed twice a day with food which was thrown on the ground. He was never allowed to use his hands for eating. Only this person, who resembled more a ghost than a human being, had the privilege of feeding those who were temporarily 'contaminated' by contact with a corpse. Only this man could contact at arm's length anyone who 'had paid the last offices of respect and friendship to the dead'.

When the time of taboo was over, the mourner could mix with the rest of the community. However, all such belongings as dishes and clothes used before the funeral had to be thrown away. But the professional feeder of mourners could never abandon his job and return to a normal life.

Flaying of the Dead

Until recently, the Hiji people who live in the mountainous border region of Nigeria and Cameroon, believed that before a corpse could be buried it was necessary to completely remove the skin from the body. This did not happen immediately after death, but following elaborate rituals.

The corpse was first placed in a sitting position on a specially constructed platform. The body remained in this position for two days. One hand of the corpse was placed in a bowl full of millet and sorghum; the other was put in a bowl of peanuts. This arrangement was to prevent the dead man taking away with him the fertility of the soil.

Before the funeral, a man, usually a member of a blacksmith clan, arrived and used his strong fingers to peel the skin from the corpse. The skin was thrown into a pot and buried in a rubbish heap.

The skinless corpse was then washed in red juice, smeared with goat's fat, dressed, and carried to a burial site.

A year after this ceremony, another rite took place in which only the sons of the dead man participated. It was a kind of ceremonial final parting at the grave of their father. The sons of the deceased would drink some spirit in front of their father's grave and pour some of this liquid on the grave, saying the following prayer: 'Here is your share of the funeral feast. Today we part for ever'.

Although the ceremonies no longer exist officially, they do occasionally take place in secret since the Hiji continue to adhere to their old religious beliefs.

Tower of Silence

Although as a rule humans either bury or cremate their dead, there are people who even today are against such treatment of the deceased. For instance, the Parsees, followers of the Zoroastrian religion, are against cremation because fire (in their belief the most sacred element in the world) might be contaminated.

In India, where the Parsees live, cremation is the most popular way of disposing of the dead. Parsees consider this a desecration. A Parsee funeral simply involves laying the dead body on iron gratings in a structure some 6 metres high, called 'the tower of silence'. It is a circular tower made of stone and has no roof. These towers are usually situated in the hills and are surrounded by trees. The stone platform on which the body is placed is divided into three rows. The outermost row is for men, the next for women, and the innermost for children.

As soon as the body is placed on the stone slab vultures appear, as if by command; they descend on the corpse and tear it up; after a time only the bones remain intact. These remains are then thrown into a central pit which is filled with sand.

A similar procedure has been employed in some regions of Tibet. The body of the deceased is placed in a special area in a deserted spot, where birds devour the flesh. The body is carried to the spot and the village men burn sandalwood. Its aroma arouses the birds living on high elevations on the rocks.

White linen covering the body is undone and the body is cut open by a special assistant to open the intestines.

After the 'invited' birds dismember the body and strip the flesh from the bones, the funeral assistant grinds the remaining bones and mixes them with barley to facilitate the birds' feast.

If the birds do not devour all the remains it is regarded as a bad sign. According to local belief, it is of paramount importance to give away all the parts of the body. As soon as this is done the soul is said to have departed the body, and the macabre ritual ends.

Fatal Number

For the Jakuna people of Sudan the number seven had such a powerful symbolic meaning that in the past their king was only allowed to rule for exactly seven years. After this period even if the ruling monarch was in perfect health he had to be put to death. The seven year period was strictly observed. If a king was killed earlier by his citizens it was believed he would take revenge and his soul would bring disaster.

The king's execution was performed by special functionaries. Two executioners worked in cooperation with one of the king's wives. The killing was performed in secret when the king was asleep or resting in bed. A hole was secretly bored through the wall to the king's bedroom. Only the king's wife knew of it. Through this hole a noose was passed to the king's wife; she quietly placed it around her husband's neck. Immediately the two conspirators standing outside the room pulled the noose tight and strangled the king. The strangulation was done from outside so as the two executioners did not have to look in the eye of the dying king.

They believed that if they did, the king's departing soul would kill them on the spot.

The ritual murder of the king was then kept secret for several months. During this time, palace officials performed their duties as if nothing had happened. And as the prolonged absence of the king could cause suspicion, talkative members of the household were informed that the monarch was unwell. One official would also impersonate the late king. If an important visitor arrived at the palace he talked to the imitated voice of the monarch from behind a curtain.

The king's heart was removed, dried over a fire and ground into powder which was secretly mixed into food. The mixture was given to the king's oblivious successor in the belief that the king's heart would make the new king strong. The king's body was then mummified by desiccation over a slow fire. The corpse was covered with tight strips of cloth to make it a mummy, and buried in an erect position.

Then it was time to announce to the people that their king had 'returned to the skies'. The burial ceremony was very elaborate. When the crowd assembled in front of the palace, the last ritual in honour of the departed monarch was performed. Special music was played and an unsaddled horse appeared with a rider and the king's mummy sitting astride behind the rider as if the king were alive. At this time, the king's body was dressed in royal coats decorated with scorpions and red birds. The feet of the dead king were in his riding boots.

While the strange horseman and the late king were performing this weird ride, the assembled people prostrated themselves, and burst out in lamentation and despair. When the rider reached the site of the king's burial, the horse had to be sacrificed. In the past, together with that of the horse, a human sacrifice was performed to ensure the king's happiness in the afterworld. Usually a slave was ritually slain. One of the king's slaves had been designated to die with the king long before the crucial seven year period had passed. Such a slave was treated almost as a king's son. Even if he was found to be guilty of a crime, he was pardoned because his guilt was said to be absolved by the master with whom he would go into the afterworld.

If the chosen slave did not show willingness to die after the king's death, palace officials would try to prepare another slave in good time for his role.

When a slave was sacrificed after the death of the king, he still played an important role in the community; special gifts were offered to the slave's ghost to propitiate him.

Winged Lion

In Bali the most elaborate celebration in honour of an individual takes place only after his death. The aim of the celebration is to liberate the soul which then is able to be reborn as another being.

The cremation usually takes place any time after the first week following the death. It is a colourful and very exciting event. No wonder it takes a long time for the family to acquire the necessary funds to organise the lavish cremation ceremony. Sometimes a dead relative has to remain buried for forty years before his remains and scrapings of the soil from his grave are taken to be cremated.

If, however, the relatives of the deceased are very poor, the corpse is carried straight for cremation without a temporary burial. In these cases, further weird customs are observed. The people carrying the corpse are suddenly attacked by another group of men. The corpse is tossed and tumbled around as the men charge on to it. While the mock fight is taking place those who struggle for the body are kept cool by the crowd who throw water on their heads. This ritual is believed to confuse the soul and prevent it from returning home to haunt the family.

Normally, however, after a long period of preparation, the body is carried to the cremation ground. It is placed inside a multi-tiered tower of bamboo, cloth, paper, and mirrors and flower decorations. The tower may be 18 metres tall and would require about a hundred men to carry it. A large tower made for a high priest or another nobleman may be so heavy that the strength of several hundred men is needed to carry it.

The different platforms of the tower represent mountains, while the flowers and leaves symbolise forests. The roof of the tower represents heaven. When it is carried, the tower is moved in circles and spun around to confuse the so-called loose spirits. This is also aimed at preventing the spirit of the deceased from finding his way home.

At the cremation site the body is transferred to a funeral sarcophagus, usually carved from a hollowed-out tree trunk and made in the shape of an animal. The animal chosen depends upon the caste of the deceased person. It is a bull for a brahman, a winged lion for a satria and a kind of an elephant-fish for a sudra.

The final stage of the funeral celebration involves burning the sarcophagus and the tower. This may take many hours. Sometimes more than one cremation is performed, and the blazes create an almost theatrical effect, dramatised by the contrast between the deep green twilight of the trees and the blaze of funeral pyres. People witnessing the ceremony are dressed in colourful garments and they are illuminated constantly by leaping flames. Occasionally they become invisible, covered by clouds of bluish smoke.

When the cremation is over, the eldest son of the deceased person or another close family member pokes through the ashes to make sure that the whole body has been burned. The ashes are finally collected and, very early the next morning, they are scattered over the sea. The priest enters the water and prays, asking the gods to order the sea spirit to carry the ashes away safely.

Although the physical body of the deceased has been completely destroyed, religious custom requires that a second cremation be performed after the main one. This time, a small effigy of the deceased is cremated in a pot. The ashes are collected and then treated in the same way as during the first cremation.

Dance with a Skeleton

No wonder the Merina of Madagascar surprise travellers with their funeral customs. These Christian people have two separate burials. The first is just simple and temporary without any ceremony. The logic of this is that the family must have time to collect money for the second burial. That is the main event. The second burial takes place after some years, by which time the body is usually reduced to a skeleton.

Relatives of the dead person exhume the body, usually a fairly shocking experience for them. The body is transported to an area near the family tomb and people gather to take part in the ceremony. Wrapped in a mat, the corpse rests initially on the laps of the close female relatives. As people arrive, the body is covered with multicoloured silk shrouds. After a eulogy, the corpse is placed on the shoulders of one of the relatives who starts an extraordinary dance with his load. This dance looks like sacrilege. The dancer shows total disrespect for the corpse. As one author notes: 'the behaviour seems to be a way of transforming and breaking the ties of the living with the individual dead. It depersonalises them and merges them with the tomb, the group and its ancestral land'.

The corpse dance is followed by a huge feast and the funeral soon changes to an amusing and joyful festival. The crowd eats and drinks. Bawdy songs are sung. It must be done this way because the lonely dead person must be entertained before the journey to the afterworld. After the celebration, the corpse is carried to the family tomb in procession.

The tombs here are extraordinarily rich compared with the houses people live in. Made of stones and decorated with arcades and balustrades the family tomb is a proud possession of Merina families. Such tombs may cost ten times more than houses and are the dominant feature of the Merina landscape. Villages may disappear, but their tombs remain intact.

For a Merina to have a happy life he has to have an assurance that after his death he will have a place in a family tomb. A man or a woman who has no such place has no right to use the community rice fields and is regarded as an outcast. The worst fate for a Merina is to be buried outside the family tomb.

The Merinas who live away from the tombs of their family often make long journeys to visit. Once every few years the tomb is opened and the skeleton is brought home to be rewrapped in new cloth and then placed back in the tomb.

Merina funerals (second ones, that is) are usually performed during the cool season of the year. Roads are overcrowded at that time as people travel to exhume bodies, or to take part in funerals.

Noisy Coffin

The custom among the Barawan people of Sarawak is that the corpse of a recently deceased person is given food and tobacco as if still alive. When a man dies, his spouse or children must in turn lie down beside the corpse and puff a native cigarette and then make the corpse smoke by putting a cigarette into his lips. After the ritual smoke, the corpse is carried into the kitchen where he is fed with cooked rice pushed into his mouth.

The body is then placed on a special chair. A plate with various foods is attached in front of the sitting corpse. While constant vigil is maintained over the dead body during the day, at night a large crowd of friends and relatives assembles near the coffin. They talk loudly, drink and eat.

Although the purpose of the noise and joviality is to entertain the soul of the dead it has another important meaning. Constant noise and light kept on at night are believed to discourage evil spirits from trying to enter the body. Sometimes a coffin emits sudden unexpected sounds which are caused by contractions of the fresh wood of the coffin. But people who are unaware of the cause are often terrified by what they suspect is the presence of evil ghosts. Immediately, action is taken and the coffin is bound strongly with rattan ropes to secure the lid. Magic plants are placed on the surface of the coffin to expel evil spirits.

An additional ritual must be observed by the wife of the dead man. For eleven days she is obliged to demonstrate her sorrow by sitting beside the corpse. She must sit in an uncomfortable position with her legs tucked under her. She wears her poorest clothes and eats only the least tasty food, which she must 'share' with the corpse. Throughout this long period of confinement, she cannot leave the corpse even for a while. She can only defecate through a hole especially made in the floor of the room.

The strong reason behind the ritual suffering after her husband's death is to deflect the supposed hostility and revenge of the soul of the dead. It is believed that the late man's envy of those who still live can only be softened by showing to him the severe hardship of those whom he loved.

After observing these rituals, the widow is obliged on every full moon to kneel alone in front of her husband's grave and sing specially prescribed hymns in his honour. This ceremony must be performed during the first few months after the funeral. During this time the widow is in constant danger that her soul can be stolen by her husband's spirit to make her accompany him to the afterworld.

Hungry Ghosts

The Chinese believe that during the seventh month of the Chinese calendar certain spirits of the dead are allowed to come back to live on earth. These spirits inhabit hell, the gates of which open at the beginning of the seventh month. As Frena Bloomfield explains, these are 'wandering spirits with no family to offer them ritual honours, those whose line has died out or who have unfilial descendants who neglect their religious duties'. These spirits are hungry ghosts and are inclined to be malicious. To appease them and satisfy their needs, people 'make offerings of joss sticks, food and paper gifts at every roadside, crossroads, temple and street corner throughout the Hungry Ghost Festival.'

Most of the spirits of the dead do not return to earth since they are offered the required ritual honours. Every traditional Chinese house has a family altar—a small shrine in the main room. On the altar are various deities and it also has the names of ancestors and in the case of the recently dead often includes a photograph. On the altar, candles are burning or red light bulbs are switched on. The Chinese make offerings of burning incense and sometimes fruit and rice grains at regular intervals to the deities.

The strangest offering was a feast in honour of the dead organised in Taiwan. Food was arranged in a most unusual way. Huge amounts of different foods were placed on a row of bamboo poles. These structures were about 15 m high and 3 m wide at the base and had a conical shape.

At a given signal the crowd rushed at the food-covered structure. As each person tried to catch a portion of the attached food from the bamboo cones, the impact was so powerful that the heavily loaded structure soon fell to the ground. Then as one eyewitness reported: 'In one wild scramble, groaning and yelling all the while, trampling on those who had lost their footing or were smothered by the falling cones, fighting and tearing one another like mad dogs, they all made for the coveted food. As each secured what he could carry, he tried to extricate himself from the mob, holding fast the treasure for which he had fought . . . Escaping quickly from the mob ready to attack him and deprive him of his precious possession, he then wildly rushed home.'

This rather peculiar way of commemorating the dead was abolished by the Chinese government in 1894.

Strangest Language

Among some peoples, even language was not a permanent feature. It changed fundamentally even during an individual's lifetime. Even the most basic vocabulary had to undergo change. An outsider who mastered the language would experience problems communicating with these people after a few years' absence.

The reason for this curious change can be found in their beliefs; when a person died it was believed his ghost would seek to do harm so all the people who had the same name as the deceased had to get new names. And the name of the object from which the man was named had to be changed. Thus, new words had to be invented almost constantly.

This custom was widespread among the Australian Aborigines. If for instance, a man belonging to one tribe of south-east Australia died, and his name was Ngnke, meaning 'water', the tribe had to use a different name for water.

Similar beliefs were held by the Goajiros of Colombia. In their case, however, pronouncing the name of the dead person was such a serious offence that it was punishable by death.

Among the Lengue Indians, not only the name of a dead man was taboo, but all the people from the community had to immediately change their own names, irrespective of what they were called before. They were afraid that death had the list of the names of all the people in the community and would soon come after more victims. But if their names changed, Death would be confused and would search for new victims elsewhere.

On the other hand, the Nicobarans (India) changed their names after a death had occurred in their community, and disguised themselves by shaving their heads, so that the ghost would be unable to recognise them.

Widow's Sacrifice

In some societies, after the death of her husband, a woman was expected to commit suicide to accompany him to the afterworld. The cruel custom was common in China and India.

In China, the sacrifice of Madam Kao was the most famous. She was the wife of Tih-O-shen and lived during the early Ming dynasty. When her husband was already on the pyre to be cremated, she unexpectedly leapt into the flames. Her attempt to die was unsuccessful because her mother rushed to her rescue and dragged her out. But the faithful widow was determined to follow her husband into the afterlife. She chewed some charred bones of her husband from the pyre, and then hanged herself.

It then became common in China for a widow to commit suicide after her husband's death, not in secret but in a ceremonial public hanging. Such a suicide and spectacle was a very expensive event. Only rich widows could afford such a suicide in public as it had to be well organised.

Once a woman made the decision to commit suicide, the exact date of the event had to be announced in good time, using special placards. Then a special stage, a kind of a raised platform, had to be erected. The platform was to be decorated with lanterns and attractive flowers.

When the widow in her finest dress arrived, she was invited to occupy a special chair near the platform. But before she took her seat it was customary for her friends to congratulate her on her brave decision to make sacrifice in honour of her husband.

The highest mandarin present then asked the widow to ascend to the platform. De Groot, who witnessed such a ceremony, reported: 'In a few moments she adjusts the fatal noose around her neck, and launches herself into eternity by kicking away a stool upon which she stands'. A huge crowd watched this self-sacrifice. After the crowd dispersed, the dignitaries who attended the cruel event approached members of the widow's family, offering them congratulations.

Suicides of widows by hanging in public had to be approved by the Chinese authorities. An order from the governor of Hukwang Province in 1832 required each widow who decided to commit suicide to apply in writing to a special Board of Rites.

The custom of widow sacrifice was also very common in India and early texts describing such an event date back to 316 AD. In one account the wife of a famous general was led to death by her brother, to the funeral pyre. She was described 'as having been all gleeful, even when the flames licked her body'.

The most detailed description of Indian widow suicide, called suttee, was published on 10 February 1735 in the *Calcutta Gazette*. The report said: 'I went ashore and walked up close to the girl; she seemed about twenty-one years of age, and was standing up, decorated with flowers . . . her clothes were then taken off, and red silk put upon her . . . She was then lifted upon the pyre and laid herself down by her deceased husband, with her arms about his neck. During the final act of the drama, a great quantity of straw and wood was laid upon her, and tar thrown on top of it. She could hear the demands from people around her to bring more fuel, and the final order to hand over the brand, with which the eldest child set fire to the straw, that was soon ablaze'.

Suttee used to be so common in parts of India that between 1815 and 1828, over 8000 widows were burned in Bengal alone.

Although banned long ago, this cruel custom has survived in remote parts of India. As recently as 1985, the Indian press reported the suttee sacrifice of a widow after the death of her husband, who was a school teacher.

'Beautiful' Death

Although ritual suicide occurs in various nations, the most famous is no doubt the Japanese hara-kiri—called in Japan *seppuku*. In this strange method of self-sacrifice a man died as a result of self-inflicting a severe wound to his stomach. This horrific method of suicide originated in feudal Japan and was mainly performed by samurai warriors to avoid capture by an enemy. It later became the method of indirect execution of a nobleman for an offence of dishonour. His death was decided by the ruling emperor who sent the convicted man a special letter called the 'death message'. In this letter the king explained in an elegant style that the man must die by *seppuku*. The letter was accompanied by the suicide weapon, a richly ornamented dagger.

On receiving the letter, the victim immediately began to prepare for the rite. It was performed either in his house or in a temple. The *seppuku* required construction of a red-carpeted dais, some 10 cm above the ground.

On the fatal day the victim's friends and certain officials of the emperor came to his house or to a temple to witness his ordeal. Wearing his ceremonial dress the victim knelt on the dais and said his last prayers. He then stripped himself to the waist and suddenly plunged his ceremonial dagger into the left side of his stomach drawing it slowly across to the right and then turning it upward.

One eyewitness noted: 'During this sickeningly painful operation he never moved a muscle on his face'. Standing close to the victim was a close friend, holding a sword in his hand. He was ready for an act of mercy. When the victim drew out the dagger from his stomach, he stretched his neck forward as if begging for mercy. At this very moment his friend 'sprang to his feet, poised his sword for a second in the air; there was a flash, a heavy, ugly thud, a crushing fall: with one blow the head had been severed from the body'.

The horrific act was ended and the bloodstained weapon used by the warrior to kill himself was sent to the emperor as proof that his will had been fulfilled with honour. The dishonour of the warrior was thus wiped out by his brave act of *seppuku*, and his family kept the right to inherit his property.

It seems strange that a method of suicide involves cutting the stomach. However, to the Japanese it is the stomach in which the spirit of a man resides and by damaging this organ the man is said to be purging all his sins.

The unusual custom of *seppuku* was initiated by Yashitsune Minamoto, a Japanese warrior in 1189 when he disembowelled himself in order to avoid the dishonour of being captured by the enemy.

Suicide by *seppuku* was a privilege of samurai warriors. To them, killing oneself in an ordinary way, for example by poison or hanging, was considered a shameful way to die. Only suicide by *seppuku* was an honourable and most 'beautiful' death. Among warriors, *seppuku* became an important tradition. Although the samurai caste was officially abolished in 1868, the custom of the most 'honourable' death did not immediately die out.

During the Second World War, many soldiers and ordinary people in Japan chose to die the most honourable death when their country was about to be captured.

Probably the most spectacular suicides were committed by selected Japanese pilots, called *kamikaze*. These young pilots dived, with their plane loaded with explosives, on to the deck of enemy warships.

The members of *kamikaze* squadrons were proud of their destiny. By the time Japan surrendered, over 4600 *kamikaze* pilots had been killed. Takijiro Onishi, founder of the suicide squadron, himself committed *seppuku* in 1945 when the defeat of Japan was imminent. His hara-kiri was, however, special. To make his suicide more painful and perhaps more spectacular, he did not invite the friend with a sword to end his ordeal. After cutting his stomach vigorously in the prescribed manner, he died after a full day of horrific suffering.

Cemeteries in the Bellies

In some parts of the world the dead were ritually eaten by their relatives. The ancient Greek historian, Herodotus reported that in some regions when old people died, they were not buried or cremated but simply eaten by their loving relatives. Reasons for such a disposal of the body varied. Eating his corpse was usually considered to be an act of sympathy towards the deceased and there was a belief that those who ate the dead body would acquire all the good qualities of the deceased person. They were eaten also to prevent the bodies from being desecrated by enemies or used in black magic.

The custom of eating bodies of deceased relatives was once common among the Kallatians, an Indian tribe. Among the Dieri tribe of Central Australia only the fat of a particular part of the dead person's body was eaten. They used to cut out and eat the flesh from the face, the belly and limbs in the belief that these parts transfer the power of the soul from the deceased.

Various parts of the body were devoured, depending on which was believed to be the home of the soul. For example, some South American tribes believed that the bones were where the soul resided. The skeleton of the dead person was burned to obtain the ash of the bones. The ash was then added to drinks for the relatives to acquire the soul of the dead. On the other hand, the Chiribachi roasted the body and collected the dripping from it. That was drunk by the dead person's relatives and friends.

On the Pannefather River, in north Queensland, Aborigines used to cut off only the soles of the feet and some fleshy parts of thighs. These were baked and cut into little pieces which were eaten later. This custom was only valid for dead children. Occasionally the mother had the right to eat the flesh of her dead child. This was done in the hope that the child's spirit would be born again through her. Even at the turn of the century such funerals were reported throughout north-west and central Queensland. But eating the child's body was the privilege only of its parents, brothers and sisters.

Certain tribes of the eastern highlands of New Guinea had a cruel manner of treating the dying. When a very old grandparent was about to die his grandsons would take him out of the house and loosely attach him to a tree branch with fibres. Forming a circle around the tree they would look at the tree top and shout, 'The fruit is ripe! the fruit is ripe!' When the man was believed to be dead they would start to shake the tree vigorously to make the body fall. The 'happy' family then seized the body and roasted it. A cannibal feast followed, during which the body was mainly consumed by younger tribe members.

Devouring corpses instead of burying them was so common in some regions of New Guinea in the past that there was a saying that 'their cemeteries are their bellies'. This horrific custom however was in some regions only confined to those who were executed after committing a criminal act. Those who consumed such a corpse believed that by doing so they absorbed the evil spirit of the dead and made it inactive, so that there would no longer be any danger to the society from that spirit.

17.

Incredible Societies

A Tribe without Children

An Angolan tribe called the Jagas hated their children so much that they killed all their infants. They justified their abnormal attitude by saying that since they were a nomadic tribe of fighters, who lived by plundering other tribes, mothers carrying infants would significantly reduce their speed of movement. Such a tribe should soon disappear, but this did not happen. The Jagas solved their problem by adopting adolescent children of the parents whom they had attacked, killed and eaten.

Large-scale killing of children was also practised by one of the Indian tribes in Brazil known as Mbaya. The only child spared was the one believed to be born last. Since the Mbaya people did not adopt any children the tribe so shrank in size that it nearly disappeared before the evil custom was finally abandoned.

On the other hand, in Polynesia in the past, the lowest social class had no right to have children. In this case the middle classes could kill their children if they liked whereas the highest social class was not allowed to do so, because these children were believed to be the descendants of the gods themselves.

Cruellest Initiation

Okipa was the name of an initiation rite for warriors in the North American Indian tribe of the Mandan. It was probably the most cruel initiation ever. In the 1830s the secret ritual was witnessed by George Catlin, an American artist who was shocked by what he saw.

To become a warrior a young Mandan had to undergo a more horrific rite than anyone would dare to inflict on his worst enemy.

Mandan tradition demanded that a young man undergo an ordeal in which he would show an enormous capacity to endure pain. Candidates had to prepare themselves for the event by refraining for four days from food and drink, and even sleep. Then, they had to come to a ceremonial hut in which the instruments of their torture were already in place. The torture was inflicted by a chief priest. He treated each man as if he were a dead animal and he himself a butcher. Using a special knife he carved slices from the man's shoulders and chest. The young candidate was suffering immensely, but this was just the beginning. The chief priest pushed wooden skewers through the bleeding wounds, just behind the victim's muscles. Firm thongs were fixed to the rafters of the hut and tied to the ends of the skewers. Then the initiate was lifted from the floor. As if this was not enough, to increase the agony, huge dry buffalo heads were fixed to the victim's legs. In this way, the candidates were suspended several feet above the ground. Each suffering victim was then spun by an attendant until he became unconscious. He was then lowered to the ground.

There was a second stage of this horrific ordeal, but not all the men could participate. Some were too sick to continue. Some candidates died of this cruel initiation.

If a novice was able to stand up he was then offered a hatchet by the chief priest. And now an even more incredible event took place. The young man chopped off the little finger of his own left hand as an additional sacrifice to the Great Spirit.

This was still not the end. In the final stage the initiate had to run in a circle like a horse with ropes attached to his wrists and with the dangling buffalo skulls still in place. This extremely painful and exhausting run continued until the novice collapsed. Each novice was left where he dropped until he was 'resuscitated' by the Great Spirit. A candidate who was brave enough to survive all these cruel tests was declared by the chief priest to be a fully fledged warrior of the tribe. He could then return in triumph to his family.

It was believed that during this painful ordeal the initiate was able to communicate directly with the Great Spirit and to acquire the power necessary for him in his future efforts to survive the dangerous life of a warrior. Unfortunately the incredible bravery and endurance of the men of this tribe were not enough to save the tribe. The Mandans prospered in the Missouri plains for many centuries where there were plenty of buffalo, but they could not win their last battle. Contact with civilisation led to an epidemic of smallpox which annihilated the brave tribe. By the 1840s only a few members survived. They were assimilated into other Indian tribes living nearby.

Monsters from Another World

The Asaro men who live in the Asaro Valley of Papua New Guinea are proud of a peculiar custom introduced by their ancestors. According to some Asaros this custom in fact enabled the tribe to survive. In the old days, when their villages were plundered by cruel neighbours, the men had to fight ferocious battles and were often overwhelmed by the warriors of certain more powerful tribes.

Fatalities from such battles were so great that the tribe was in danger of being exterminated. The warriors of the attacking tribes were particularly interested in killing all the male children, in an effort to prevent the tribe from gaining the upper hand in future battles.

In this situation, when the fate of the whole tribe was at stake, one of their wise men invented a strange method of fighting in disguise. He organised a secret meeting of the warriors and ordered them to make special preparations before the coming battle. Each warrior had to cover his head with thick white mud. When it dried it would be impenetrable to enemy arrows. These unusual head covers had eyes and nose and ears made in the shape of a ferocious beast.

When a group of the Asaro warriors were about to attack, they looked as if they were monsters from another world. No wonder that when the Asaros arrived in their disguise for the first time, the unsuspecting enemy became so terrified that they even forgot to defend themselves. The Asaro mudmen took advantage of their highly effective armoury and for many years terrorised the entire region. Their secret military strategy was passed on to their offspring. The tribe became strong and prosperous.

Soon they began to cover their entire bodies with a thick coat of mud. Thus their bodies became impenetrable to their enemies' weapons.

It has since become customary among the Asaros to wear a special head covering of a bamboo frame coated with white or grey mud.

Such coverings can be used often and are often decorated with pig tusks so the face of a warrior resembles the face of a pig. Some coverings were modelled so as their expression was really horrific.

The tradition of making head coverings was so strong that even with the change of their life-style in recent years, the Asaro men are still proud of their famous disguise. This time though, they make their famous head coverings to attract tourists. The covers they make nowadays are about 2 cm thick and shaped in the form of a large bowl. Holes are made for eyes and mouth while an extraordinary nose and huge ears are made separately and then attached to the cover. To make the face even more frightening, the mouth is often fitted with human or cuscus teeth.

Weird Taboo

In some societies such a common human activity as drinking and eating was subject to strict taboos, not only on ordinary people but even on kings. In the Loanga kingdom of West Africa there was a custom that no-one could see the king eating or drinking. It was believed that otherwise he would immediately die. The belief was so strong that when one king's twelve-year-old son, whom he loved greatly, by accident saw him drinking, the father ordered his son to be slain. The body of the king's son was cut into small pieces which were then displayed during a special procession, with the proclamation that he had to be punished because he had seen the king drink.

Great precautions were taken to prevent servants seeing him eating or drinking. If while there were other people in the palace the king needed a drink, a cup of wine was brought by his servant. Immediately, the servant had to turn his face. The servant made a signal by ringing a bell so that all present could fall down with their faces to the floor. They remained in that position until the signal that the king had finished drinking.

Similar customs were practised by the Banyoro people of Central Africa. When their king visited a dairy and wished to drink some milk, men had to leave the room immediately, and all the women present had to cover their faces. This peculiar taboo applied even to domestic animals. One day when his favourite dog entered the palace room while the king was eating, the dog had to be immediately killed.

In some regions, the taboo on seeing a man eating or drinking is observed by ordinary people, who all eat and drink in seclusion. Anthropologists who have studied these peculiar customs say that they had to bribe people if they wanted to see them eating or drinking.

Eating in seclusion may be the result of fear that the evil eye of an envious or hungry or thirsty person may bewitch the food or drink.

Opposite was the custom practised by the Kefans. They were only permitted to eat or drink in the presence of other people. Some chiefs of the community employed special servants to be ready to witness them drinking or eating. Even when a chief was ill and wanted to drink his medicine during the night, he had to call his servant to witness.

Mysterious Resurrection

A very strange initiation ritual to adulthood for boys, known as Nanda ceremony, used to be performed in Fiji. The ritual was carried out in a special sacred ground constructed far away from the village. It was a huge stone circle, 30 metres long and 15 metres wide. The stone wall was about one metre in height. The structure was called Nanda, which literally meant 'bed'. Just before the initiation ceremony a large amount of food was stored. Special cabins were built near the enclosure.

On the chosen day, novices were led in a single line by a priest. Each boy held a club in one hand and a lance in the other. When the procession reached the vicinity of the Nanda, it was met by several old men of the community gathered in front of the walls, singing ritual songs. The novices stopped. Each of them dropped his weapon just at the seniors' feet. This was regarded as a demonstration of their respect. The clubs were a symbolic gift. All the boys then entered the cabins, where they had to remain for five days.

On the fifth day, the boys were again led to the sacred walls of the enclosure but there was no-one waiting for them. This time they were allowed to enter the sacred ground. In the enclosure the astonished boys saw a row of men, lying down, covered with blood, their bodies cut open and their entrails protruding. The boys concluded that these men had been massacred. The priest who guided the initiates then walked over the bodies. The confused and terrified boys had to follow until they reached the other end of the row while the chief priest watched them.

Suddenly, with a terrific yell all the 'dead' men jumped to their feet and ran to the river; they then cleaned off the blood and 'decorations' and filth.

The men who disguised themselves as corpses represented the ancestors who were suddenly resuscitated by the mysterious power of the rite, a power in which all the initiates could share. The purpose of this grisly scenario was not simply aimed at terrifying the young men during their initiation to adulthood, but at showing them the mystery of death and resurrection in the sacred enclosure. This was a great experience for those entering the life of adult men. They were taught by the priests that death is never final and that the dead always return.

Potlatch

To help themselves to achieve high rank in the community most people try constantly to increase their wealth. But in some communities the opposite was true. Among the Kwakiutl Indians living on Vancouver Island, the way for a man to achieve high status was to give away or destroy his most valuable possessions in front of a watching crowd.

This was done during a special ceremony of 'giving' called the potlatch. Potlatches were only organised to commemorate important events such as the marriage of a nobleman or the birth of a son to a chief. Hundreds of spectators gathered to observe this peculiar ceremony and to listen to the speeches of those who were boasting about how many valuable possessions they would give away or destroy. It was in fact a kind of competition, usually involving two sides.

According to the witness of one such potlatch, that took place in the 1890s, one of the competing chiefs poured hundreds of litres of precious fish oil on the fire in his efforts to 'defeat' his opponent. In response, his rival threw several wooden boats and hundreds of blankets on to the fire. The fire got so huge that it endangered the community hall. The destruction of the canoes greatly impressed the spectators. Little wonder, since building a canoe required the hard and long work of many people.

In one case, when a Kwakiutl chief saw that he had no more valuable objects to destroy during a potlatch, he took one of his slaves and beheaded him. He substantially increased his chances of winning the contest.

But the greatest sacrifice of wealth for the Kwakiutls was the breaking of a copper plaque. They were considered to be the most desirable form of property and a plaque, which was beaten out from lumps of copper ore, had immense value. One plaque could buy twenty canoes and twenty slaves. Each plaque even had its own name, as though it were human. But the waste of a plaque during a potlatch was extremely rare.

In the long history of the potlatch competitions some men won by burning down their only house in front of the spectators.

It was necessary to destroy or give away valuable goods but participants also had to show complete lack of concern at the enormous losses.

The potlatch tradition continued into the 1950s. By then, Kwakiutls were giving away not only home-made goods but manufactured goods such as television sets.

A Map on the Head

The Yanomamo, who live in the tropical forests of Southern and Northern Brazil, have the reputation of being about the most violent people in the world. They fight almost constantly with neighbouring tribes, ambushing and killing them, and their behaviour is really unpredictable. Violence and cruelty are practised from early childhood, and even during times of peace, the Yanomamo men do not stop fighting; instead they organise duels and competitions among themselves.

Most of the duels and outbreaks of violence are caused by disputes over women, who are in very short supply. And the main objective of their warfare is to capture women from neighbouring villages. The village men are killed, but the women are captured alive and often raped on the spot. Then they are taken back to the Yanomamo territory where they are offered for pleasure to any warriors who did not participate in the raid. The captured enemy women then become wives of the Yanomamos.

The shortage of women was the result of a strange custom of the Yanomamo men. Their first-born child must be a male. If a girl is born first she must be secretly killed in the forest by the mother just after birth. The Yanomamo women kill their first-born daughters and the secret killing goes on until the woman presents her husband with a male infant.

One of the most popular competitions among Yanomamo men is the so-called pounding competition. In this event two men show their power by inflicting and receiving powerful blows from an adversary. The event is eagerly watched by women and children assembled in a central clearing in the village. The men barrack · for their fighting colleagues.

Two men take position, opposite each other. Then, the fight commences. According to one eyewitness: 'Leaning back, one of them puts his entire strength and weight behind his clenched fist as it thuds against the target's chest'. The blow is so powerful that the struck man 'staggers, knees buckling, head shaking, but silent and expressionless'. The scene is repeated and more blows follow until it is the receiver's turn to hit at his opponent. Although this competition is very painful, participants eagerly volunteer to take part in order to gain a reputation for being strong and fierce.

A higher level of Yanomamo competition in violence is so-called club fighting. This is even more dangerous. A man challenges his adversary over some dispute, and arrives for the duel carrying a 2-3 metre long pole. The challenged man sticks his own pole of the same size in the ground and leans on it. He bows his head as if inviting a blow. The adversary takes his pole by the thin end and hits his opponent's head. The blow seems hard enough to crush the skull. The hit is sustained without a word though. The receiver is now allowed to hit his opponent back. The duel continues and the watching crowds yell with excitement. The show is over when one of the participants cannot stand any more. Sometimes these individual contests develop into fights involving axe or stone duels and result in severe bloodshed or even death.

Small wonder, with such methods of demonstrating their bravery and fierceness, that the head of a Yanomamo warrior is covered with long ugly scars. Yanomamos are very proud of the scars because they are evidence of their masculinity. In fact they shave the tops of their heads and paint them with red pigment to highlight the scars. An adult Yanomamo warrior may have twenty such scars on his head. They resemble a road map.

Civilisation of Honey

The main occupation of the Guayaki tribe of eastern Paraguay is finding nests of bees and making sure that they have enough honey to eat. Honey is the tribe's main food. From morning till night, they wander in small groups in the forest.

Their knowledge of bee behaviour is unparalleled. First they look for bees laden with pollen and find out which direction they fly in. The Guayakis follow the bees to their nest, hidden high in the forest. They use smoke to avoid being stung by the bees, but they often find 'friendly' bees belonging to *Melipona* species. They have atrophied stings and do not sting. They are ideal targets for hunters of honey.

To reach bees' nests in high trees is not easy. The Guayaki use a scaffold of ropes and they climb the trees with truly acrobatic skill. The ropes they use are made of vegetable fibres combined with human hairs and are very tough.

Having reached it, the tribesmen use stone axes to open the nest. They collect honey combs into large baskets. They collect wax too and use it for a variety of purposes. They even mix wax with clay and use it as a glue for moulding small utensils.

Guayaki men are excellent climbers but the honey collecting is risky and some hunters die for the honey in the forest.

Members of one scientific expedition which explored the regions inhabited by the Guayaki tribe once noticed with surprise a man hanging on a tree top in the forest. At first they thought he was alive, but they found later that he had died long ago. The corpse was hanging on a thick rope attached to the tree. He had one hand broken, and the other was still inside the bees' nest.

Stone Money

When we have a lot of coins in our pocket or purse we sometimes complain that our money is heavy and inconvenient to carry. But our money is extremely light compared with the money used by the people of Yap island, (Micronesia).

Imagine a single coin weighing five tonnes. The huge Yap coins may be over 3.6 metres in diameter. With a Yap coin of 1.5 metres diameter, you can buy several houses or even a small village. All this for just a single coin. The Yaps also have small coins of just a few inches in diameter.

Larger coins have to be kept outside the house. The islanders say that a large stone coin cannot be stolen because everybody knows who owns it at any given time. Strangely, some big coins are better known to inhabitants of the island than people. The people are born and die but their great stone money remains there from one generation to the next.

Each coin has a hole in the centre. A bamboo pole can easily be put through, and the pole carried on the shoulders. If a coin is very big, two men carry each end of the bamboo pole.

When a very large stone coin of several tonnes has to be moved, a long beam is put through the coin's hole. A hundred men would be needed to perform the job.

For a big project, for example, constructing several houses for which a large sum of money is required, the stone money is paid but does not need to be moved. It is used to pay the bill, but remains exactly where it was. The owner of the huge coin changes. During the past three hundred years, one big coin has had many different owners but the coin has never moved. And there is no need to move it as everybody knows who owns it.

The Yaps do not worry about it being stolen by a well organised gang from overseas as they know their stone money is useless outside the island.

Once, an Irish-American trader, Captain O'Keefe, started selling the Yapis huge stones of crystalline limestone from the island of Palau, 200 miles from Yap. At first he was paid with fish and copra. But later the captain demanded the most attractive women in exchange for his cargo. The clever trader could make huge money selling the Yap women in Hong Kong; the most beautiful he kept as his own wives.

When the Germans assumed control over Yap Island, the captain was charged with polygamy and threatened with life imprisonment. This scared him, so the story said. He stocked his schooner for a long voyage, kissed his beautiful wives goodbye and sailed away. He was never seen again.

The stone money is still in use today, although US dollars are used in most ordinary transactions on the island.

Blood Drinkers

Some of the most famous and admired inhabitants of Africa south of the Sahara are the Masai of Kenya and Tanzania. Their herds of cattle are their proudest possessions. The men look especially attractive; their slender and long-limbed bodies have been admired by Europeans since time immemorial.

The Masai have some truly strange customs. When a child is

born, visiting women who come to admire the new-born child, are supposed to spit on the floor; otherwise evil forces may attack the baby. When the baby's teeth develop the mother pulls out the first two front teeth in the lower jaw to make the child more attractive.

Until recently the Masai had the custom of extending the ear lobes. Rounded weights were attached to the ear lobe of a child and eventually stretched the lobes so much that they could reach the shoulder.

A custom among the Masai of the Dorobo tribe is that after circumcision a boy walks around the village in search of young girls. He carries special arrows and a bow. He shoots at each girl he meets. The arrows do not cause any harm as they are blunt, but the strange hunting shows officially that he is now interested in girls.

Initiation takes place some time later and after that the young man becomes a warrior called a moran. He is a moran for seven to fourteen years. During that time he is not allowed to marry. He can however engage in unrestricted sexual intercourse.

Later, during the marriage ceremony of a moran, the other men of the same age-group have the right to enjoy sex with the bride. In fact, the bridegroom would be dishonoured if one of them refused. Throughout the marriage, according to strong Masai tradition, all members of the husband's age-group can demand their right to have sex with his wife. She cannot refuse.

Probably the most peculiar custom of the Masai is that they are regular blood drinkers. Every day they drink fresh blood drained from their cattle. They simply shoot an arrow at the cow's vein and the squirting blood is collected in a gourd. The arrows are tipped with a small block of wood to ensure that they do not penetrate too deep. The blood is usually drunk mixed with cow's milk.

The Masai also have rather unusual funeral customs. Only very important persons of the tribe are buried. They are put in a very shallow grave. To show respect the person is provided with a new pair of sandals.

But generally the Masai have a great fear of the dead and believe that a dead body will contaminate a hut. Whenever a person is about to die or is hopelessly ill but still alive, they are removed from the village. Often, an old and dying father or mother, still fully conscious, is carried away by his children. Placed far away from the hut in the savannah the dying person is left to breathe his last without ceremony. He or she has no power to fight and becomes the easy prey of scavenging hyenas. Although it is very cruel, this 'funeral' custom still prevails in some areas.

Golden Stool

A year-long national rebellion once took place over a piece of furniture. This is the story of the Golden Stool of the Ashanti people of Ghana. The stool was the most precious possession of the Ashanti people and nobody, even the king, was allowed to sit on it. To the Ashanti, it represented the spirit of the nation; according to Ashanti legend, the Golden Stool floated down from the sky in a cloud of dust.

But the British did not understand the significance of this stool. In 1900, British forces conquered Gold Coast, and the commander of the forces and governor of the new colony, Sir Frederick Hodgson, demanded that the famous Golden Stool be brought to him so he could sit on it.

His demand was very provocative: 'Where is the Golden Stool? Why am I not sitting on the Golden Stool at this moment? I am the representative of the paramount power. Why did you not take the opportunity of my coming to Kumasi to bring the Golden Stool and give it to me to sit upon?' No more insulting request could have been made to the assembled Ashanti chiefs. No wonder they rebelled against the British. It was a year before peace was re-established.

Even then, the British governor sent secret missions to the Ashanti region to find and bring out the famous stool. The missions failed because the Ashanti kept the stool in a secret place in deep forest. It was constantly guarded. All the bloodshed would have been avoided if the British had known more about the history and traditions of the Ashanti nation and the particular importance of their Golden Stool. Finally, when the British stopped their efforts to secure the Golden Stool, the Ashanti stopped fighting.

The famous Golden Stool is important because it is a symbol of the whole nation, but there are many other stools which are also of special value to the Ashanti. They are not gold or silver, but simple wooden stools. They are kept in each Ashanti house. It is believed that the soul of an ancestor is embedded in the stools after his death.

Stools are treated with veneration. In a special ceremony held in honour of an ancestor, water is poured on the ground in front of the stool to ritually 'wash hands'. Yam, called 'soul food' is ritually offered. In the old days it was customary to sacrifice a sheep for the occasion. Its intestines were smeared on the 'sacred' stool of the ancestor.

Banana Ritual

In the forested regions of Montaña in Peru lives a tribe known as the Amahuaca. They have a fascinating ritual linked to the banana and aimed at making their offspring strong. During harvest festival, the men sit together and chew the soft outer flesh of ripe bananas to form a pulp. This is spat into large pots. To the pot is added the harder inside of the fruit which has been chewed and spat out by the women. The whole brew is then boiled until a lot of steam is produced.

Children are swung back and forth through the steam in the belief that it will make the children strong. The brew is then drunk by the men.

And the rite goes on. To further enhance their strength, each child is carried by two men to the edge of the forest. The men who have previously swallowed a lot of brew, now vomit it over the child's body. Similar ceremonies are performed in a festival during the maize harvest, but in that case the mixture is merely spat over children's bodies.

The obsession with strength is so great that the rituals are even performed at funerals. The body is cremated in a special pot. The left-over bones are picked up and pounded in a mortar, and mixed with a maize soup. This drink is then consumed by all the relatives in the belief that it will give strength.

According to the Amahuaca, the strength of the dead man will pass on to the survivors and ensure that the spirit called yoshi will not attack them. They treat yoshi as a spirit which is often ill-disposed to people and the spirits, they say, wander in the forest, occasionally attacking people.

They distinguish between male and female yoshi and say that a woman may have sex with a male spirit in the forest. But the result of such intercourse is a very ugly child, which must be killed by the mother.

The most feared among the yoshi is the female yoshi called 'wantati'. They say that it is a woman whose vagina is lined with sharp teeth. If a man sleeps with such a yoshi, his penis is bitten off.

Human Sacrifice in Africa

Human sacrifice is usually associated with ancient Mexican civilisations, but most people are unaware that people in some regions of Africa also practised human sacrifice. But while human sacrifice in the New World was performed to please the gods, in Africa sacrifice was not necessarily a religious duty.

In some African kingdoms in the past, it was believed that when the king died he had to be commemorated by human sacrifice. In Benin (Dahomey), when the king died at the beginning of the eighteenth century, hundreds of people were slain to serve him in his afterlife.

According to a British officer, Captain Snelgrave, four hundred prisoners were killed during this Grand Sacrifice in 1727. All the king's many wives were sacrificed, too.

The last Grand Sacrifice took place in 1860 to commemorate the death of King Gezo. The cruel ceremony was witnessed and described by a Frenchman M. Lartigue. Six hundred victims were slain over two days. He reported: 'As a finale, the late king's wives placed themselves in order of rank around his body . . . and drank poison, so that this voluntary sacrifice brought the number of victims up to six hundred'.

The skulls of the victims were placed in the form of a pyramid or were used to decorate the walls of the king's palace. Apart from the huge human sacrifice at funerals, there were the so-called annual customs in which new victims had to be sacrificed to provide the late king with fresh servants in his afterlife. Many fewer victims were required, though.

One such annual sacrifice was witnessed by Sir Richard Burton in 1863. 'Only' twenty victims were killed. Burton said that he had seen the appointed victims before the execution: 'all were seated on stools and tightly lashed to the interior posts; each had an attendant squatting behind him to keep off the flies. They were fed four times a day and were let loose at night to sleep, since the king wanted to keep them in good humour'.

There were many other sacrifices, too. The king often needed to send messengers to communicate with his father's ghost. This always required a human death. Any event of significance had to be reported to the ancestor spirit, so, some such trivial event as the visit of a white man, or even a new type of drum had to be reported and each such event required a messenger.

As one traveller explained: 'a single message to the late ruler could result in several deaths. After one victim was beheaded to carry the news, the king would suddenly remember that he had forgotten some minor detail. In order to add a postscript to his letter another courier was slain and sent to the next world'.

Sacrificial victims were also a must when the king was about to engage in a war. And when a new palace was built it was customary to bury several victims under its foundations. The victims' blood was mixed with clay and used for the palace walls.

Leopard Men

Early in the seventeenth century, white explorers brought back incredible stories of the so-called Leopard Men of West Africa. Disguised as leopards they attacked and devoured innocent people. Such accounts were ridiculed and remained a travellers' tale till the end of the nineteenth century.

In 1897 the British colonial authorities in Sierra Leone became troubled by increasing numbers of sinister killings in the forest. They decided to investigate. They discovered a powerful organisation in the region called the Human Leopard Society. It was responsible for the ritual killings, but acted in such secrecy that for a long time it was impossible to catch the members. These criminals really did dress like leopards and their main murder weapon was a peculiar three-pronged knife.

Finally one of the Leopard Men was captured and the whole truth about the incredible organisation emerged. Most of the Leopard Men led normal family lives and only rarely at night would a member become a Leopard Man—a ritual killer. When ordered by the chief of the organisation a Leopard Man would not hesitate to attack and slay even a close family member. To be fully disguised, he painted leopard-like spots and whiskers on his face and attached metal claws to his hands.

The Leopard Man would attack the victim while he was walking alone in the forest. The Leopard Man would overpower his victim and use his 'claws' to tear out the jugular vein, killing him on the spot.

Sect members of the society waiting nearby would come and

quickly remove the body to a secluded area of forest. There a macabre ceremony took place. The heart, liver and intestines of the victim were cut out, and the rest of the body was cut into small pieces so that it would be impossible to recognise.

The Leopard Men claimed that the killings were ordered by their ancestors when the well-being of the community was threatened. For example, when the chief had died and the men quarrelled about who should be the next chief, the quarrelling greatly weakened the village. To restore 'health' to the community the ancestors would order the killings, to frighten the people into making a quick decision about who should be the next chief.

18.
Magic and Sex

Copulation Magic

Among the Western Enga people of Papua New Guinea an adult cannot survive without knowing and using magic.

A man cannot even have sex with his wife without first learning the magic that will protect him from the dangers associated with marital sexual intercourse. He must also know magic to destroy the evil effects of his wife's menstruation.

He must refrain from having sex with his wife for at least a month after the wedding ceremony. He needs all this time to learn the appropriate magic from an older, married, relative. The teaching is not provided free of charge. The husband, who is still wearing bachelor clothes despite the wedding, pays his teacher a fee of a new net bag containing a cowrie shell and cooked pig's guts.

Only after the teacher is convinced that his pupil has fully mastered the magic does he allow the man to have sex with his wife. As famous anthropologist, M. J. Meggitt explains: 'On the way the couple perform a ritual in which they plant an iris and a taro in a secluded plot to ensure a long and prosperous married life. Then as the husband prepares for copulation, he spits on his hand, rubs his belly and mentally utters a spell to prevent the loss through ejaculation of the vital juices in his skin. After the pair have visited the forest several times, they doff their wedding dress and settle down to married life. Some men say that the husband needs to practice his copulation magic for only a year or so; others insist that he should continue until the birth of his first child'.

Compulsory use of magic is not confined to men. A menstruating woman can never afford to forget to cleanse herself magically since she is extremely dangerous to others. Widows and unmarried girls (that is, those women who do not engage in sex), have only to employ relatively simple magic but not so the married women. As Meggitt elaborates: an unmarried woman 'recites a spell and paints white crescents under her eyes (and sometimes a stripe from navel to pubic hair). But such treatment is inadequate for a married woman. On the fifth morning of her seclusion, her husband faces the rising sun and bespells a small pocket of *Evodia* leaves and *Setaria* grass which he sends to her. She bites off the ends of the leaves; the remainder of the packet she may either burn, place in the house-gable to rot, or bury with her menstrual pads of moss. Then she puts kaolin under her eyes and is free to resume her normal activities'.

Killing someone by employing magic was rarely done among the Enga. But, when the cause of death was uncertain, a specialist was employed to do an autopsy. As Meggitt notes: 'If, however, there is no indication that the death followed from old wounds, the expert seeks evidence of sorcery. He examines the interior of the heart and lungs for black marks. Marks in the right-hand cavities demonstrate that a living member or ghost of the deceased's patriclan killed him with sorcery; marks on the left-hand side point to a maternal kinsman or ghost. This information is sufficient for the two groups of relatives to agree on the payment of compensation. No attempt is made to ascertain the actual identity of the sorcerer'.

Most of the all-purpose magic is known by men. They learn magic by inheritance or by buying it. Magic is used for a wide range of purposes. It is employed for instance to have a successful hunt for pigs. Young people employ magic to promote their growth or to improve their external appearance.

Queen with Many Wives

In the north of South Africa there was an unusual kingdom known as Lovedu, ruled by the so-called Rain Queen. The queen did not have a husband but she had wives. They were young girls and they lived in her palace. The wives had sexual relations with a male royal genitor, and when children were born they called the queen 'father'. The children were regarded as brothers and sisters to each other. They all lived in the palace as one large family, and there was no rivalry for the throne.

The queen was said to possess the powers to make and withhold rain and cause locust plagues. Nobody dared to attack her kingdom. Even the immensely powerful Zulu army avoided her.

Because of her incredible power it was believed that the well-being of the queen was vital to the prosperity of the kingdom. She was thought to be immune from disease, and unlikely to die from any mortal weakness. It was said that if she were to die suddenly people would flee in fear of imminent famine. In other words, when the rain-queen dies 'the country dies with its owner'.

It was customary when the queen became old, for her to perform ritual suicide by taking a special poison which contained among other things the brain of a crocodile.

The queen's death was not announced but was kept secret for many days. People continued to arrive at her palace, seeking her advice or arbitration.

The queen's body was rubbed to collect some of her skin to be used as an ingredient in the rain medicine for her successor lady queen.

She was later buried in a most peculiar way. Her body, wrapped in cloth, was kept standing upright, and facing north. Her ancestors came from this direction.

Her body was gradually covered with soil but the head was left uncovered for about half a year until it had completely decomposed.

19.

Healing By Magic

Elixir of Six Thousand Human Hearts

The medicine men of Africa acquired a great deal of knowledge concerning the use of native plants to cure illness. But in some African societies the most powerful medicines were obtained from human flesh. These medicines were procured by cutting the flesh from the body of a living person. Anyone chosen for such a rite had to be slain later.

The British authorities had great problems in their attempts to eliminate the ritual killings, the sole purpose of which was to use human flesh for making medicine.

Although medicine men usually obtained flesh from prisoners of war, innocent strangers were sometimes captured. Occasionally even a guest at a party could become a source of medicine.

One such case was reported in Lesotho in 1948. A guest invited to a party was suddenly overpowered, and stripped by the men present. They started to 'collect' the guest's flesh by cutting off small pieces of it. The victim could not defend himself.

One abductor even collected the victim's blood in a special dish. The abductors looked for fleshy parts, cutting from the calves of the victim's legs, from his biceps and a portion was cut from his breast and another from his groin. All the pieces of flesh were collected in a white cloth and displayed before the medicine man. Then the whole face of the victim was cut off and his throat was cut to end his incredible agony. The corpses that had been carved like this were first hidden and after a certain period of time carried to a remote place and left exposed to scavengers. Magic medicine made from such macabre materials was used to cure serious illnesses and even as a poison to make enemies ill.

In some parts of Africa in the past, hearts of enemies captured in battle were eaten raw to magically fortify a warrior's courage.

A tribe living on the River Orinoco in Venezuela had a most unusual method of preparing magic medicine from a human corpse. The corpse had to hang for several days in a hammock and all the 'fluid' which dropped from the body was collected. This 'fluid' was believed to be a most powerful medicine.

When the king of Arakan in Burma ascended to the throne in 1634, he was warned by one of his prophets that he would die soon after the coronation ceremony. Then it was revealed by another of his advisers that the king could be saved if he would drink a special elixir. It was an unusual elixir. It had to be a concoction made of six thousand human hearts mixed with two thousand hearts of white doves. Nevertheless the magic ingredients were obtained, the story says, and the medicine given as advised, but the king died anyway.

Spirit Toys

Folk doctors are widely used by the poor or less educated strata of Mexican society. Methods of diagnosing and curing patients vary with the healer and the illness. A disease may be diagnosed for instance by 'cleaning' the whole body of the patient with an egg, which is then broken into a saucer. If the egg liquid resembles a snake shape it is concluded that the culprits are spirits of the air.

The prescribed treatment could be a massage with warm herbal lotion and oil on two consecutive days, performed by the practitioner. On the third day the patient might be asked to take a hot bath in a special herbal potion. The treatment concludes with beating the patient with a branch of moist leaves. After leaving the 'clinic' the patient has to throw the branch in a particular stream.

Sometimes, however, such treatment does not work because the spirits of the air stubbornly refuse to leave the body. Then the spirits have to be bribed, with gifts. The spirits seem to have childish inclinations as the gifts are supposed to be little toys made of clay and dough. They take the form of small dolls, toads, snakes and various other creatures. All kinds of delicious foods should be offered as well. This is to be attractively arranged in baskets decorated with crepe paper of brilliant colours. The practitioner then takes the baskets to the place where the patient was attacked by the spirits and leaves them there. He or she begs the malevolent spirits to leave his suffering patient.

King's Magic

During the Middle Ages in some European countries people believed that kings were not only rulers but healers. They claimed that certain incurable diseases such as scrofula could be cured by the magic of the king.

The king did not need any sacred medicines. It was enough for him to touch the sick person with his fingertips. The king would touch the most painful part of the sufferer's body and then give the patient a coin. Each person touched by the king received the so-called 'Touch Piece'. It was then worn to remind him of the king's 'miraculous' treatment. Some greedy people even exploited this custom by making several visits to the palace to get more coins. Some royal touching ceremonies were arranged with great pomp; others were very simple.

This medical practice of kings was initiated in England in the eleventh century by King Edward the Confessor. He was famous for his sensitivity to human suffering.

The custom of healing citizens by the king was then imitated in France, by King Philip I (1060-1108). In both countries the custom persisted for centuries.

Each king's successor maintained that his miraculous power to cure by touching had passed to him from his predecessors.

In England, the most famous healing king was King Charles II. It is said that after his return from exile in 1660 he was able to touch some 90 000 sick people during his 22 year rule.

There is no evidence as to how effective this royal touching was, but the custom persisted in England till 1688 when it was finally abolished by King William of Orange who considered the method of healing useless. When sick people surrounded his palace, the king got angry, but asked his servants to give them some coins and demanded that they go to doctors.

The custom of healing by the power of king's fingers was practised in France much longer. It was in use on and off, until the 1780s. The magic of kings' fingertips has now vanished for ever.

20.
Killing By Magic

Bone Pointing

Belief in the power of a medicine-man is so strong in some societies that he is able to kill at a distance without poison or a weapon. The power of his magic spell is so strong that there is no escape for those he decides to punish. Such black magic is known to Australian Aboriginal medicine-men. They use a special technique known as pointing the bone. The medicine-man jabs a sharpened bone in the direction of his victim, usually with strong thrusts or twists as if showing the harm to be inflicted on the victim's body.

Ethnographers were reluctant to believe reports that people could die as a result of black magic employed by Aboriginal medicine-men. But one case was studied in detail. In 1956 a young Aborigine from the Northern Territory angered his elders by breaking an important taboo. They held a ceremony during which an invited medicine-man pointed the bone at the guilty man. By the time a medical doctor arrived to help him, the man was already in very poor shape. He was unable to stand and his body seemed to be paralysed. His breathing soon became difficult. He seemed to be dying.

To rescue him from inevitable death the man was attached to an artificial lung. His breathing then began to improve. His condition gradually improved and he started eating and drinking. He soon recovered. When asked what happened to him he explained that once the iron lung began to work the old magic faded away.

Although the man had almost been dying when admitted to the hospital there was no trace of any illness. Psychologists declared that the young man had been subject to a very powerful and effective form of self-suggestion.

Blinding 'Medicine'

Belief in the power of magic was so strong among the Banyoro tribe of Uganda, that it was used as a weapon in battle. Whenever there were reports that an enemy was about to start an assault, they immediately used the magic weapon. This was in fact a special medicine. It was supposed to make the enemy warriors blind, and incapable of further fighting.

It was made from the flesh of a blind animal. A blind animal, such as a calf or a puppy with its eyes still closed, had to be found. The 'blind' animal was then ritually killed by the local shaman who prepared the magic medicine.

The animal's flesh was cut into small pieces and mixed with ordinary food so that no-one would recognise the magic involved. The medicine was then divided into very small portions which were secretly buried under every road or path that enemy troops were expected to use. The hidden medicine became the Banyoros' magic line of defence. They believed that when an enemy warrior walked over the hidden medicine, he would be struck temporarily blind.

The belief certainly improved the morale of Banyoro soldiers, so the unusual medicine had its value. It was said that as soon as the 'blinding' magic was employed the Banyoro could successfully defend their land by the force of their spears and arrows.

A different tactic was used by the Bechuana tribe of southern Africa. Instead of using magic to blind their enemies, they used magic to make themselves invisible to their enemy. The magic was used when the warriors were ready to attack a neighbouring tribe. Just before the battle a medicine man was invited. With a woman assistant he performed the magic rite in front of the assembled warriors.

First the shaman's woman assistant ran in front of the warriors with her eyes shut and waved a huge fan as she shouted the magic formula: 'The army is not seen'. This call was then repeated by the medicine man who sprinkled all the warriors' spears with a potion made of magic plants and other secret ingredients.

Then the second part of the rite was performed. This involved the magic 'blinding' of a black bull. Using a thread taken from the bull's tail the animal's eyes were blinded by sewing up its eyelids. Then the 'blind' bull was driven in front of the waiting troops where it was ritually slaughtered. Roasted and cut into small pieces the flesh was offered to each soldier to eat. The rite was believed to make the soldiers magically invisible during the coming battle.

Moving Corpse

The strong belief among the Australian Aborigines was that only a very old man or an infant could die a natural death. Other deaths, they claimed, were always caused by black magic. Even if a victim died from the fatal blow of a club during battle, it was said that black magic, applied by a wicked man, made the blow fatal. Nearly every death, therefore, had to be avenged.

Close relatives of the deceased person first tried to find out who the culprit was. Since the victim's spirit always wanted revenge, it was thought he would help identify the murderer.

The family usually invited a native doctor to perform an inquest. He was thought to be especially well qualified for this. Odd methods were employed by the medicine man. For example, he examined the ground around the victim's grave, and from the arrangement of the soil he determined the direction in which the murderer lived. Or, he could sit near the grave and 'see' the spirit of the culprit. He could also dream information about where to look for the murderer.

Some tribes employed other tactics. Aborigines living near the Lower River Murray made the closest relative of the murdered person sleep with his head on the corpse before burial. It was thought that the spirit of the deceased would give him a useful hint about the murderer in a dream.

Another method was used by the Malngin people of the eastern Kimberleys. They used the victim's bones to reveal the identity of the murderer. The victim's bones were pounded finely, and mixed with food. This was then offered during a special feast to which the person suspected of the crime and many other guests were invited. It was believed that when the culprit swallowed the secret meal it would choke him, revealing him as the guilty person.

Even stranger methods of detection were used by Aborigines living in the northern parts of South Australia. It was their custom to place the corpse of a murdered person on the head of three men. Then, names of various neighbouring hostile tribes who were suspected of the crime were spoken. The corpse was supposed to 'jump off' their heads as soon as the name of a guilty tribe was mentioned.

Magic Tobacco

In some cultures, smoking tobacco is not just a pleasure but an essential part of religious life. The Warao Indians of the Orinoco delta of eastern Venezuela believe that their Supreme Spirit must be nourished by tobacco smoke. They claim that if their shamans neglect their duty and stop producing large amounts of smoke, the Supreme Spirit will become offended and bring calamities and death to all in the region.

The shamans are, therefore, obliged to smoke almost constantly. And to produce a lot of smoke they use extraordinary cigars each containing several rolled tobacco leaves. One such cigar can be 75 cm long.

People believe that by ritual smoking a shaman is able to directly contact the Supreme Spirit and this provides him with unusual power over the people. Shamans are held in great respect and are believed to be vengeful if offended. If a powerful shaman becomes angry it is believed he might produce serious illness in his adversary and may even kill by hitting his enemy's body with a malevolent magic arrow. They claim that one shaman could swallow a piece of glass or other sharp object and make it into a magic arrow to enter the body of a victim and make him sick.

A shaman is also a healer. He is believed to have the power to extract the 'arrow of sickness'. He is usually summoned to treat a patient at night when tobacco smoke can easily be seen. He simply places his hand on the affected part of the body and then magically sucks out the 'arrow of sickness'. He inhales a large quantity of tobacco smoke, and pretends that the arrow of sickness now travels through his arm and then through the exit hole in his hand, propelled by the smoke. Although nobody can see the malevolent arrow the watchers believe that it travels in the ball of smoke.

21.

Incredible Magic

Creating a Crocodile

One of the strangest rituals in Australia was performed by the Aborigines of the Kendall River district on Cape York Peninsula. They believed that they could create crocodiles. In fact the making of crocodiles took place at the same time as the initiation ceremony of sixteen-year-old boys.

An old man was responsible for creating the crocodiles. The procedure was as follows. The man took a baby lizard and saturated it with blood from the arm of a youth. He then threw the blood-soaked lizard into the river. It was believed that this lizard grew into a crocodile which would become blood brother to the youth.

As Bill Beatty noted in 1952, the youth was beautifully decorated for the occasion: 'His scarred and mutilated body is painted with daubs and streaky lines of red and white ochre. Hanging from his ears are strings of shark and crocodile teeth. Bracelets of shells and teeth adorn his ankles. On his head he wears a headdress of beautiful, many-coloured parrot and cockatoo feathers'.

Because of the blood-brother relationship with crocodiles, the Aborigines of the area were friends of crocodiles and it was said that these dangerous beasts never attacked them.

Belief in the ability to create certain beings was not only confined to Aborigines of Australia. It is still believed in Tibet that by sheer willpower a local magician can create a being called a tulpa, which is a product of his imagination, and yet becomes real and can be seen by everybody.

A French journalist, A. David-Neel, after studying Tibetan magic for a long time, claimed that he was able to create a tulpa figure of a monk who was his house companion. After a few weeks, however, the Frenchman got tired of the figure. But at first, he was unable to dematerialise him. It took him about six months before he succeeded. It seems of course, that the Frenchman must have been mentally unstable or had a trick played on him.

Men Who Turn into Horses

In Jakarta in Indonesia not long ago, visitors could witness a peculiar ceremony called a Horse Dance. It was a ceremony organised in a house known as a 'spiritual healing sanctuary'. The ceremony began with a group of some twenty men reciting spells. Then one after another all these men begun to change their behaviour. It was such a dramatic change that it was hard to believe that half an hour before they had been ordinary people.

The men began to behave like horses. Folco Quilici, who witnessed the ceremony, noted: 'The hysterical repetitions of the magic words were like explosions, the music was overbearing and obsessive; and the piercing gaze of the leader of the group, the medium, was irresistible'.

The transformation was gradual but evident. Although, at first, only one man behaved like a horse, there was no mistaking the transformation of behaviour: 'They neighed and pranced, and when they were offered hay from a basket they ate it. Like spirited steeds they frothed at the mouth and kicked. They drank thirstily and ate more hay until they fell to the ground exhausted. The crowd, which had been silent up to that moment gave a great shout'.

During the dance the 'horse-men' were accompanied by a group of masked men who represented the evil spirits responsible for causing illnesses to humans. To the sick who witnessed the peculiar ceremony, and who strongly believed in the power of magic, such transformation of men into horses was a great shock. As it is believed that a horse is a symbol of strength it was thought that the horse is capable of defeating evil demons and removing the cause of illness.

Men who turned into horses were believed to have the same miraculous power to expel evil spirits. This was why the Horse Dance was performed in a healing sanctuary.

Human Skull Magic

The human skull played an important role in magic medicine, as it was believed that medicine made of a human skull would cure epilepsy, considered in the Middle Ages to be of supernatural origin.

A special elixir known as Spirit of Human Skull was once popular in England. Only the unburied skull of a convicted criminal could be used. There was such a demand for these skulls that local apothecaries made special contracts with executioners.

King Charles II was an enthusiastic user of skull-derived medicines. A special preparation made of chips of human skull bone mixed with spirit and wine was administered to him when he was seriously ill. (It did not help.)

As late as the nineteenth century, in Ireland, special 'old' skulls with lichens on the surface were in high demand. Scrapings of skulls with the greenish lichens were sold in the belief that they had exceptional medicinal properties.

In fact, according to medieval magicians, the skull is the centre of human psychic power and they included skulls in their sacred rituals.

Belief in the special value of the skull led to various burial customs in which the skull alone was treated with special respect. The other parts of the body were discarded. Some of these traditions have even survived. The most curious is still practised in the Austrian village of Hallstadt in the region of Salzkammergut. According to the custom which is said to have originated in the fifteenth century, human skulls are excavated from the graves every fifteenth year to be decorated. During the special day all bodies from the churchyard are removed and the skulls are separated from other skeletal remains which are put back in a crypt. The skulls are cleaned thoroughly and then painted by a special artist who specialises in this. On each of the skulls the name of the deceased person is written, as well as his or her date of birth and the date of death. In addition, an emblem signifying the occupation of the deceased person and his or her gender is painted on the skull. If the deceased is a priest, a cross or an open book is painted on his skull. For a young girl the emblem is usually a rose. On the skulls of those who died as a result of, for example snake bite, a snake is painted. All the decorated skulls are then put on a large shelf where they can be seen by the public.

A different method of skull decoration was practised by the Arara Indians of South America. They kept skulls as their trophies and they were decorated to make them look more attractive. Each skull was decorated with feathers and the lower jaw was held in position by a special cord.

The Power of Spells

A number of strange methods was used by magicians to influence the people. One of the most popular ways was to make clay or wax models of the intended victim and stick pins into these models. This custom was practised in England, and with minor modifications was practised world wide. Another way of doing harm by magic in England was to rub unpleasant substances into the victim's clothes. These substances included goats' urine and toads' venom. However, the most popular method of inflicting harm was by casting a spell. To do so a magician had to say appropriate magic words. It was often written in a book of magic which was hidden. It had to be consulted in a mysterious place—for instance in a forest at midnight.

Surprisingly, among the Chinese casting a spell is not confined to magicians. Ordinary people can buy spells and their use is so common that special shops sell ready-made spells. These spells are usually written on black or red paper which is considered to be lucky paper. Spells are even used for minor problems, such as to cure headaches, or in order to drive away mosquitoes or to keep away burglars.

If a person has a serious problem, he usually goes to a temple where he consults a medium who examines the problem and finds a solution by preparing a written spell. Such a spell can be either put under his pillow when he sleeps to make it effective, or the person can burn the written spell and swallow the ashes. Such 'eating' of the spell is most popular in Taiwan and Hong Kong.

While many spells used cause no harm to other people and are believed to be most effective, there are some spells the aim of which was to inflict harm on others. Such traditional black magic exists even now in Hong Kong. Such magic is called Hak Tao which means black path, and the practitioners of this magic are known as Little People Hitters. These are usually old women.

When someone wants to act against his enemy, for example, his own boss, he can visit the Little People Hitter who will punish him magically by sending a harmful spell. Such wicked services only cost a dollar or two in Hong Kong and the woman Hitter can be hired for a day for about ten dollars.

A Hitter would then write down on a piece of paper the name of the person to be punished. She then 'sets fire to it and starts beating out the flames with the slipper,' while offering the incense to the evil spirits, whom she is calling upon to punish the 'guilty' person whom she calls the Little Person. The spells are said not to cause any major harm or death but they are believed to cause minor accidents or other unpleasant situations to a person on whom the spell was cast. People strongly believe in the effectiveness of such spells and there are many stories to support this among even the better educated Chinese.

Termite Oracle

Among the Azande people of Central Africa the guilt of a man accused of witchcraft or murder is often decided by chickens. The Azande are strongly convinced that through the chicken the oracle always reveals the absolute truth. In fact, many innocent people die because of the verdict of the chickens.

This strange oracle, however, is not only consulted in the case of a crime but also consulted to find the prospects of a planned hunting expedition or whether a business undertaking will be successful.

Very often the oracle is consulted by men who suspect their wives of infidelity. They say that a straying wife 'can escape the eyes of men but she cannot escape the eyes of the oracle'. And the oracle, can only be consulted by men.

In this weird form of judgement chickens are fed with a powerful poison and the fate of the chickens indicates the answer of the oracle. Both the questioner and the operator of the rite have to abstain from sexual intercourse for a few days before the test.

Two fowls are used. The test is usually carried out in a secret part of the forest. Holding the beak of one fowl open the operator forces it to swallow the poison. Then the questioner asks the oracle whether the suspect is guilty of his or her crime. If the chicken dies, it is considered doubtful. To confirm the verdict another chicken is fed with the same poison. If the next chicken survives the guilt is confirmed. If both chickens die or both survive, it is said that the oracle has refused to give an answer. The oracle must be asked again during another session.

Although the poison oracle is regarded as reliable, it is an expensive way of determining guilt. The plant from which the poison is prepared does not grow in the Azande region and a six day journey is required to collect it.

To remedy that problem the Azande have discovered another oracle which does not need poison. Instead, the minute blind inhabitants of termite hills are consulted. The termite oracle is popular and is called the poor man's oracle. It can be used by both men and women, even by small children. No poison is involved.

The termites are usually consulted towards the evening. Having found a termite mound in the forest a man, using his spear, opens one of the shafts into the mound and inserts two sticks taken from two different trees. The termites provide answers to Azande questions, according to whether or not they eat the sticks.

An old man may for example inquire whether he will die soon. He asks by saying the following: 'O termites. If I will die this year, eat the branch "dakpa" [the first branch used]. If I will not die eat "kpoyo" [the second branch]'.

The results are expected the next morning. If the second branch inserted has disappeared or is partly damaged and the other untouched, the man is happy as it means that he will not die. If both branches are eaten it signifies that either the taboo was broken by the questioner or the witchcraft of another man has interfered with the test. If neither of two branches has been eaten, the termites have refused to give their verdict. The disadvantage of this poor man's oracle is that only one question can be asked at a time and the answer takes hours to obtain.

Another form of magic is used to detect and punish adultery. When an Azande man suspects his wife of adultery, he smears his penis with magic medicine before having sex with her. The poison then enters the woman's body but will not cause her any harm. Neither will it harm the husband because he has taken an antidote. But if a lover sleeps with her the poison will attack him and cause severe, even fatal, illness.

The Magic of the Oath-stone

Black magic has probably never achieved such a high level of sophistication as in the Kenyan secret society called Mau Mau. It was a truly incredible organisation. Its members belonged to the Kikuyu, the largest tribe in Kenya. The aim of the organisation was to ritually kill the white settlers in the fertile highlands. The existence of the group first came to the attention of the outside world in the 1950s, when many white settlers became victims of Mau Mau.

The chiefs of the Mau Mau recruited their members in such a way that they remained absolutely loyal. The unusual oath taken by the candidate, to become a warrior in the war against the white colonists was: 'I swear that if I am ordered to kill, I will kill, no matter who it is. In the event of my killing anyone, I will cut off their head, extract their eyeballs, and drink the liquid from them. When I go to kill someone, I must take with me a strangling rope, a small knife to extract the victim's eyes, and a handkerchief to cover my hands against fingerprints'.

The oath taking was linked with magic too. The medicine-man used powerful magic to ensure that the vow would not be broken. A special stone with seven holes represented seven orifices found in the male's body; that is two nostrils, two ears, a mouth, anus and the penis. While the oath was being taken the medicine-man poked a stick into each of the holes to ensure that the words of the oath would not escape from the stone. The oath ceremony concluded when a candidate called upon the oath-stone to magically kill him and bring death to all his family members if he broke it.

Expulsion of Evil Spirits

In many cultures in the world people used to believe that all calamities are the work of evil spirits; no wonder many methods were used to keep them away.

Expulsion of devils was common in Ghana, where a special ceremony was organised every year to drive away the evil spirit called Abonsam. One such ceremony was described in 1844 by an Englishman. He noted: 'As soon as the eight o'clock gun fired in the fort the people began firing muskets in their houses, turning all their furniture out of doors, beating about in every corner of the room with sticks . . . and screaming as loudly as possible in order to frighten the devil. Being driven out of the houses, as they imagine, they sallied forth into the streets, throwing lighted torches about, shouting, screaming . . . rattling old pans, making the most horrid noise, in order to drive him out of the town into the sea'.

Before this noisy expulsion, for four weeks people behaved so as to deceive the devil. There was no talking in the streets, no shouting, no singing nor playing instruments. It was a period of total silence. If people started to quarrel in the street they were arrested and heavily fined. Even when someone died people were not allowed to weep or mourn loudly. The belief was that the silence would be noticed by the evil spirit. At first he would be puzzled by this unusual silence. Then later, an unexpected horrific noise would frighten the evil spirit so much that he would flee. In one part of Ghana they even killed all the roosters because it was believed their crowing showed the expelled evil spirits the whereabouts of villages.

Among the Huron (North American Indians) the expulsion of evil spirits involved breaking and knocking over everything they came across in their huts.

In Cambodia, in some regions people used to believe that demons lived in pieces of broken statues and stones. To expel the demons all these pieces were collected and brought to the capital. Huge elephants were used for the rite. When a large number of elephants were assembled, guns were fired to frighten and stampede them across the shards and pieces.

The elephants were said in this way to expel the demons from the town. To make sure all the evil spirits were frightened enough to escape, the ceremony was performed on three consecutive nights.

On some of the Nicobar Islands a model of a ship with sails was made. It was carried through all the villages of the region in the belief that the evil spirits would board it. Then the ship of ghosts was floated out to sea by the village men. While the ship sailed away, the excited crowd shouted: 'Fly away, devil, fly away, never come again'.

People on the coast of Guinea used to believe that they could force evil spirits to enter effigies of people and animals. These images were usually made of wood and were placed at the entrance to every hut. On a chosen day, at about 3 o'clock in the morning, the people made as much noise as possible to force the evil spirits to enter the effigies which were then thrown into the river.

Sometimes driving away evil spirits must be performed because of an epidemic or other disaster. People do not wait for an annual festival. When a calamity occurs the people of Minahasa in the Celebes leave their homes and move to temporary huts erected solely for this purpose. They stay there for several days. They completely empty their homes. They carry all their belongings with them. Some days later all the inhabitants return to the village in absolute silence. They approach their homes slowly in order to arrive unnoticed by evil spirits. On a signal by their priest the people start yelling and start hitting doors and windows with wooden sticks to frighten and drive away the evil spirits. To make sure that none of the spirits returns, the priest makes so-called holy fire.

Mysterious Magic Cult in Japan

A number of magical cults came into being after World War II. The strongest was founded in 1960 by Okada Yoshikazu. It is called True-Light-Supra-Religious Organisation. The cult has about two hundred temples. Members of the cult claim that they possess the skills to stop disease, revive the dead and repair broken appliances, all by magic.

Winston Davis, who investigated the organisation in the 1970s found many examples of successful magic. The magic was sometimes the result of the use of a special amulet which is said to transmit the 'spirit rays' of the force of purification. The possession of this amulet is very important. There are special instructions regarding its handling. It can only be removed when its owner is naked and it cannot be hung on a nail with another amulet. Otherwise its 'wavelengths' are confused. If it is accidentally dropped, head office in Tokyo must be immediately contacted since as a result of the fall it will probably have been disconnected.

In isolated regions of Japan there are still shamans called miko. They use trance to communicate with the guardian deities and spirits of the dead.

The most famous shaman to claim extensive occult powers was no doubt Deguchi Onisaburo who founded the Omoto religious movement in Japan. In 1898 he began claiming that he travelled extensively in both Heaven and Hell. On his journey he was granted magical powers such as second sight, meaning that he could see as far back as the time of the creation of the world. During his travels he was 'killed, split in half like a pear with a sharp blade, dashed to pieces on rocks, frozen, burnt, engulfed in avalanches of snow and turned into a goddess' and yet he was able to return to his old self and reach the centre of the world.

During World War I he claimed to be an incarnation of Buddha. During his life he dictated eighty volumes of writings. His sect still exists in Japan.

Crocodile Judge

Fear of crocodiles was utilised by one famous witch-doctor in a small village near Tamale in northern Ghana. For a magic cure the doctor used the crocodile as a therapy. While the doctor talked to a patient, especially one who suffered mental problems, the door would suddenly open and a big crocodile would appear. The patient was of course saved by the doctor and this shock therapy usually worked. Unfortunately, in 1966 the witch-doctor himself was devoured by his 'assistant' crocodile.

In many parts of Madagascar crocodiles were considered to be a symbol of wisdom and good judgement. There even used to be a peculiar form of judgement called 'ordeal by crocodile'. The accused person submitted himself to an ordeal in which a crocodile could kill him or spare him. If the crocodile judge considered him not guilty he did not attack him. This however rarely happened.

Walking Dead

Haiti is the home of some incredible customs which have led to many disputes among travellers and anthropologists. In the 1920s Dr Antoine Villiers, a French physician who for many years worked in Haiti brought home stories about zombies, that is dead men brought back to life by certain local shamans called bokors.

Since then many stories have been published of people buried long ago but occasionally seen alive. In 1939, for instance a report was published by Zora Hurston of a young girl found alive four years after she had died and been buried. When discovered, she was working as a slave in a local shop. The girl was recognised by her relatives especially because of the distinct scar on her foot.

Despite such reliable information, the scientific world remained sceptical. Small wonder, as it was rather unscientific to accept that a person who is supposed to be dead and buried can be seen walking around, alive.

It was therefore surprising when a scientific report appeared in one of the journals in 1983 describing in detail a real case of zombification in Haiti.

In 1963 a young man was treated in a local hospital for a mysterious disease. He was soon declared dead by two physicians. The body was given to his family and he was buried in a local cemetery in a ceremony witnessed by relatives and friends. Imagine their great shock, when twenty years later, a middle-aged man approached a woman in the town and introduced himself by the nickname of her deceased brother. The man claimed that many years before he had been changed into a zombie by a sorcerer. He claimed to have worked for many years as a slave on a remote sugar plantation until the death of his boss freed him.

This unusual case was thoroughly investigated by doctors and police and confirmed as true. We know now that the shamans use special poison. When applied directly to the skin of a healthy man it causes a mysterious disease. The victim's breathing deteriorates so much that it is almost undetectable. The heartbeat ceases almost completely. The man soon looks dead and even an experienced doctor would not hesitate to pronounce him dead.

But the man does not die. He is in a deep coma. During it he retains consciousness and is fully aware of what is going on around him. He can hear his relatives crying during preparation for his burial, but being paralysed by the poison he can do nothing. When he is finally put into the grave he is still alive and he can survive on the small amount of air in the coffin.

At a chosen moment when nobody is around, the victim is dragged from his grave by the shaman's assistants. To make him fully alive the zombie maker gives him a secret potion. Under the influence of this hallucinogenic drink the newly resurrected man is in such a state of shock that he has no power to protest and follows the orders given by his tormentors. Having experienced his own death, burial and mysterious resurrection, the man who is now known as a zombie, is usually secretly sold as a slave. Such a zombie is aware that his sudden appearance in his home village may frighten people to death, so he usually works out the rest of his life on a remote sugar plantation and does not try to escape.

The poison used by Haiti shamans for making zombies is a clever mixture of the pufferfish, which is among the most toxic fish known, and the highly poisonous *Datura* plant.

Baron Samedi

One of the strangest 'religious' cults in the world can be observed among the inhabitants of Haiti. Although cult members claim to be Christians they have added to it their former pagan deities, making a new religion known as voodoo. Their religious ceremonies begin with Christian hymns but include blood sacrifice and ecstatic dances.

In their festivals they display elements of magic which their ancestors brought from their motherlands in West Africa. They are in fact descendants of Negro slaves who were shipped to Haiti in the seventeenth century to work on sugar plantations.

In very early days the voodoo cult required sacrifice of humans at the altars of their temples, and their rituals involved human blood drinking followed by sexual orgies. No wonder some European historians described the Haiti inhabitants as 'blood-crazed and sex-crazed savages'.

Voodoo devotees believe in the existence of many deities which they call loas. They say that a loa is always willing to help people when they are called on by those who venerate them. If the deities are not worshipped in a proper manner, they may become offended and severely punish people.

Among the most feared is the loa of death and resurrection called Lord of Death or Lord of the Cemetery. It is a very peculiar deity. It is portrayed as a gentleman called Baron Samedi. It always wears an old-fashioned suit, a top hat and a pair of glasses. Although it may seem to look ridiculous in a contemporary society this deity is most terrifying for voodoo-worshippers and they make efforts not to disobey him.

As a Lord of Cemetery and Lord of Death this deity is chiefly venerated during All Souls Day. On that day a flock of local women gather at a local cemetery to pay their tribute to the deity. Dressed in black and purple dresses, they sing and dance for many hours in honour of Baron Samedi who they believe is always present on such occasions. To please their strange deity, the women's dances soon change to lasciviousness, and each woman holds a stick representing a mock penis.

The most interesting rite is the voodoo service conducted in a temple. The service begins in the evening and involves a lot of dancing. A breathtaking account of one voodoo service was brilliantly presented by Kyle Kristos: 'But now some of the dancers are falling into odd positions. Their limbs move spasmodically and a strange look has come into their faces. The pupils of one woman's eyes have moved under her lids so that only the whites are showing. A few specks of foam have appeared at the corners of her mouth. She jerks and twitches uncontrollably and suddenly falls to the ground'.

According to voodoo worshippers the weird behaviour of the

dancing woman signifies that she is being possessed by Baron Samedi. The woman is immediately carried to a special room where she takes off her clothes. She is then dressed in long trousers and a man's jacket as well as a top hat so that she begins to resemble Baron Samedi. The woman is now believed to have become fully possessed by the god. She is brought back to the main hall of the temple where she is greeted by voodoo worshippers as Baron Samedi.

The ceremony continues and exactly in the middle of the night an animal sacrifice is performed in honour of the Baron Samedi and other loas. Chickens and roosters are usually chosen but sometimes even a goat is brought for the occasion. The animals are thoroughly washed with water and then perfumed with fragrances.

Ritual killing of the animals then takes place. The head, heart and liver as well as feet and intestines are removed and displayed in a big jar as the offering to the loas. The remaining parts of the animals are cooked and eaten by celebrants. There are unconfirmed reports that among some voodoo sects human sacrifice was practised in secret not long ago.

Voodoo worshippers can be possessed by loas as well as by Baron Samedi. As a rule each devotee has a particular loa who can possess him if he wishes.

Worshippers possessed by the snake god called Damballah behave like a snake. That is, they wriggle and writhe. Those possessed by the deity of love display erotic behaviour.

A woman possessed by Ghede, the god of the phallus, would exhibit male sexual behaviour, showing intense sexual attraction towards other girls, even trying to rape them.

Index